THE YOUTH
MINISTER'S
SURVIVAL GUIDE

ZONDERVAN/YOUTH SPECIALTIES BOOKS

Professional Resources
Called to Care
Developing Student Leaders
Feeding Your Forgotten Soul
Growing Up in America
Junior High Ministry
High School Ministry
The Ministry of Nurture
Organizing Your Youth Ministry
How to Recruit and Train Volunteer
    Youth Workers (Previously released as
    Unsung Heroes)
Youth Ministry Nuts and Bolts
The Youth Minister's Survival Guide

Discussion Starter Resources
Amazing Tension Getters
Get 'Em Talking
High School TalkSheets
Hot Talks
Junior High TalkSheets
Option Plays
Tension Getters
Tension Getters Two

Special Needs and Issues
The Complete Student Missions Handbook
Divorce Recovery for Teenagers
Ideas for Social Action
Intensive Care: Helping Teenagers in Crisis
Rock Talk
Teaching the Truth About Sex
Up Close and Personal: How to Build
    Community in Your Youth Group

Youth Ministry Programming
Adventure Games
Creative Programming Ideas for Junior High
    Ministry
Creative Socials and Special Events
Good Clean Fun
Good Clean Fun, Volume 2
Great Games for City Kids
Great Ideas for Small Youth Groups

Greatest Skits on Earth
Greatest Skits on Earth, Volume 2
Holiday Ideas for Youth Groups
    (Revised Edition)
Junior High Game Nights
On-Site: 40 On-Location Youth Programs
Play It! Great Games for Groups
Super Sketches for Youth Ministry
Teaching the Bible Creatively
The Youth Specialties Handbook for Great
    Camps and Retreats

4th-6th Grade Ministry
Attention Grabbers for 4th-6th Graders
Great Games for 4th-6th Graders
How to Survive Middle School
Incredible Stories
More Attention Grabbers for 4th-6th Graders
More Great Games for 4th-6th Graders
More Quick and Easy Activities for 4th-6th
    Graders
Quick and Easy Activities for 4th-6th Graders

Clip Art
ArtSource™ Volume 1—Fantastic Activities
ArtSource™ Volume 2—Borders, Symbols,
    Holidays, and Attention Getters
ArtSource™ Volume 3—Sports
ArtSource™ Volume 4—Phrases and Verses
ArtSource™ Volume 5—Amazing Oddities
    and Appalling Images
ArtSource™ Volume 6—Spiritual Topics
Youth Specialties Clip Art Book
Youth Specialties Clip Art Book, Volume 2

OTHER BOOKS BY LEN KAGELER
Discipleship for High School Teens
    (Christian Publications)
Helping Your Teenager Cope with
    Peer Pressure (Group)
Short Stops with the Lord
    (Christian Publications)
Teen Shaping: Solving the Discipline
    Dilemma (Revell)

THE YOUTH MINISTER'S SURVIVAL GUIDE

HOW TO RECOGNIZE AND OVERCOME
THE HAZARDS YOU WILL FACE

LEN KAGELER

ZondervanPublishingHouse
Grand Rapids, Michigan
A Division of HarperCollins*Publishers*

The Youth Minister's Survival Guide

Youth Specialties Books, 1224 Greenfield Drive, El Cajon, California 92021,
are published by Zondervan Publishing House, 1415 Lake Drive, S.E.,
Grand Rapids, Michigan 49506

Library of Congress Cataloging-in-Publication Data

Kageler, Len, 1950-
The youth minister's survival guide : how to recognize and overcome the
hazards you will face / Len Kageler.
p.   cm.
Includes bibliographical references.
ISBN 0-310-54341-X
1. Church work with youth. I. Title.
BV4447.K354 1992
253'.2—dc20   91-668
                                                                          CIP

Edited by Margery Squier and Kathi George
Designed by John Flynn, F2 Design
Typography by John Flynn, F2 Design

Printed in the United States of America

92 93 94 95 96 97 98 99 /   / 10 9 8 7 6 5 4 3 2 1

ABOUT THE YOUTHSOURCE™ PUBLISHING GROUP

YOUTHSOURCE™ books, tapes, videos, and other resources pool the expertise of three of the finest youth ministry resource providers in the world:

- **Campus Life Books**—publishers of the award-winning *Campus Life* magazine, who for nearly fifty years have helped high schoolers live Christian lives.

- **Youth Specialties**—serving ministers to middle school, junior high, and high school youth for over twenty years through books, magazines, and training events such as the National Youth Workers Convention.

- **Zondervan Publishing House**—one of the oldest, largest, and most respected evangelical Christian publishers in the world.

Campus Life
465 Gundersen Dr.
Carol Stream, IL 60188
708/260-6200

Youth Specialties
1224 Greenfield Dr.
El Cajon, CA 92021
619/440-2333

Zondervan
1415 Lake Dr. S.E.
Grand Rapids, MI 49506
616/698-6900

To Clyde
. . . for his long-haul commitment to
young people and youth pastors

To Steve
. . . for showing me it's possible
to be a youth pastor
to your own children

To the Congregation of
North Seattle Alliance Church
. . . who has hung in there with me
since 1978

CONTENTS

FOREWORD by Jim Burns 11

PREFACE 13

Part I: Good Times and Hard Times Ahead

Chapter One   Long-Term Youth Ministry:
                     Worth the Effort 17
Chapter Two   Moving In, Moving Up, Moving Out 25
Chapter Three   Caution: Conflict Coming 37
Chapter Four   Competency and Compromise 49

Part II: Essential Skills: Building Fences Against Failure

Chapter Five   Working Positively with Your Pastor 63
Chapter Six   Working Positively with Parents 75
Chapter Seven   Working Positively with Kids 87
Chapter Eight   Management 101 99
Chapter Nine   Management 102 109
Chapter Ten   Avoiding Seduction 121
Chapter Eleven   Blueprints for a Five-Year Stay 131

Part III: Knowing When to Leave; Learning How to Stay

Chapter Twelve   What to Do If the Ax Falls on You 147
Chapter Thirteen   Reading the Signs: When Is It Time
                     to Leave? 157
Chapter Fourteen   The Renewed Youth Worker 167
APPENDIX A   Survey of "Fired" (or "Forced Resignation")
                     Youth Pastors 177
APPENDIX B   Sample Schedules 183
APPENDIX C   Six-Year Curriculum Plan 189
APPENDIX D   Youth Survey (Fall) 193
APPENDIX E   Performance Appraisal Questionnaire 195
ENDNOTES   199

FOREWORD

Developing a youth ministry reminds me of a story about a father who was accused by his young son of never paying attention to him or to what he did. The father felt rotten, so one day he retrieved a picture from the back seat of the car that had been scrawled in crayon. The little stick figures were simply labeled, "The Family."

The father was touched and had it mounted and framed. He took his son into his office and there among the degrees, honors, and plaques was the simple picture of "The Family." The child was stunned into silence. Finally he turned to his father and said, "It's nice, but why would you want Freddie Cohen's picture of his family hanging in your office?"

I don't know about you, but when it comes to youth work I sometimes feel like this father. No matter how hard I try to do it right it seems like I am always coming up a little short.

Youth work isn't easy. Just when you think you are figuring out how to minister to kids, an angry parent shows up at your door complaining that your youth group is far too "religious," just after your pastor mentioned to you this morning that the group wasn't spiritual enough. I recently told my wife, Cathy, "Spending time with kids is great. It's all the other stuff that drives me crazy."

The Youth Minister's Survival Guide is exactly what the title claims to be. This book, like no other book written on youth ministry, will give you practical, insightful advice from one of the best. It's a book that will help you *thrive* much more than only survive this wonderful call from God to work with his kids. This book covers the basics in youth work. The advice is sound, and no one can read this book without becoming a better youth worker.

I see Len Kageler on every page of this book. He has built a solid, practical youth ministry that has affected hundreds and hundreds of kids and families over the years. He is one of the few veteran youth workers I know who not only has a magic touch with kids, but also does an outstanding job managing his ministry. Through the years he has taught many of us a great deal about building fences against failure and how to last in youth work over the long haul.

Vince Lombardi's famous advice about football goes the same for youth ministry: "When you get away from the fundamentals, you've gone a long way toward defeat." Thanks to Len Kageler we have a wonderful fundamental book that will keep our ministries flourishing for years.

Jim Burns, President
National Institute of Youth Ministry
San Clemente, California

PREFACE

I've wondered for a long time why some people last in youth ministry while others get washed out. I have been in some kind of youth ministry job since 1969 and have seen literally hundreds of youth workers quit or get fired.

This really began to bother me when I came to North Seattle Alliance Church. As I settled in for a long-term stay, I really began to notice how quickly youth workers cycled through the churches in the area. Like tellers at a local bank . . . they'd be here today and gone tomorrow. I'd build a friendship with another youth worker, and woosh . . . he (or she) would be out the door. I felt sad because I missed the friendship. If I was hurt by their leaving, what must their youth group members feel?

With all these feelings simmering in my cerebral stew, I finally decided to do some real research. My church was kind enough to give me a three-month sabbatical, and *The Youth Minister's Survival Guide* became the major agenda item.

I phoned all over the country and found no denominational office or college/seminary youth ministry department that tracks these things. Since I had been a sociology major in my undergraduate days at the University of Washington and had nearly finished a master's degree in it at the University of British Columbia after seminary, I welcomed the chance to do some credible research—particularly on youth pastors who have been fired.

You will find my survey and its results listed in Appendix A. Throughout the book the findings are interwoven. As you read and see a statistic that is not footnoted, it means the numbers came from my research. Actual quotes from the survey respondents appear in *italics*. And, of course, all the names of the fired youth pastors have been changed.

A word about sample size. No, I didn't have the budget or the time to come up with 5,000 cases, though I am sure that many do exist. My case file grew, one by one, as I phoned around the U.S. and Canada asking people to fill out the survey. If you've ever gone to a university library and thumbed through the social science research abstracts, you've noticed that most studies make conclusions based on twenty to forty cases. I have 175 sad cases here . . . real people who have lost their jobs as youth workers.

My cases do not represent interviews I have conducted. I asked people *who knew people* who had been fired to fill out my survey, recalling as best they could the particulars. Weeding out duplicates was easy since the survey asked for the fired person's initials and church denomination.

My concern in *The Youth Minister's Survival Guide* is to provide a valuable resource for youth workers. Just as important as the survey results, I have learned many things the hard way over these years in youth ministry. A few times I've nearly quit myself, and twice I've had people crusading to get me fired. These difficult experiences would have been at least a little easier to bear had someone more experienced told me what to expect and how to respond.

My sincere prayer is that some of the joy and some of the pain shared here will be both an encouragement and a help to you.

Len Kageler

PART ONE

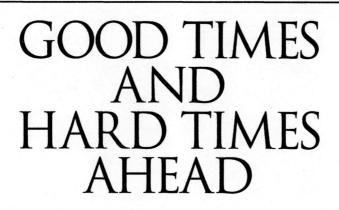

GOOD TIMES
AND
HARD TIMES
AHEAD

CHAPTER ONE

LONG-TERM YOUTH MINISTRY: WORTH THE EFFORT

John fingered the swizzle stick in his hot chocolate and finally sighed, "Well, next time I'll be smart enough to ask about the pastor's track record."

His pastor had fired him only three weeks before. Shortly afterward he learned that this pastor had fired quite a few youth pastors. In fact, the pastor normally fired a new youth pastor after eighteen months. John had done some checking . . . the man had been firing youth pastors like this for fifteen years.

I'd heard a lot of horror stories, but this one really shocked me. "So what was his excuse this time?" I asked, amazed.

"Insubordination." There was a long pause and finally he continued. "It's his normal way. He trumps up charges of disloyalty, the board is in his pocket, so his word goes."

"He must be totally insecure."

John agreed, "I now clearly see what I didn't notice at first. This guy's gotta be in control and get the praise. Anyone else's success is a threat."

I went back to my cabin with quite a mix of feelings. I love youth pastor retreats and had looked forward to this one for almost a year. It had been a good night. I even won a game of "Risk." "Ruler of the world" in less than three hours . . . yes . . . it doesn't get much better than that! I had soundly defeated my global foes, in Christian love, of course. I love playing "Risk," and I love winning even more.

I felt sad, too. John was hurting and I was mentally giving speeches to the pastor who had fired him. "What a total jerk" was among my kinder thoughts. I was also feeling sad because several of my friends were missing. They weren't missing because of a wife having a baby, a youth group member in jail, or an important meeting with their volunteer staff.

They'd been fired, too! It wasn't a very good year for our group of youth pastors. Ben lost his job because he spent most of his time trying to win unchurched kids, and parents of the church kids felt their sons and daughters deserved better. Larry, like John, couldn't get along with his senior pastor. The ax fell with the words, "Your strengths are not in the areas we need, so it's time for you to move on." I suppose if you're going to get fired, it's nice when they give you the bitter pill with a little jam, too.

And what about JoAnn? Her career ended after only fourteen months because the kids just didn't like her. Discontent, seeping upward as sure as capillary action in a ninth-grade science class, had spread to the parents and finally to the board. The boom on JoAnn was lowered with the words, "It's obvious you do not have the right gifts to be a youth pastor. Please have your office emptied in two weeks."

I was sad because others were missing from the retreat, too. Jeff and Dennis had left youth ministry for the greener grass of being "senior pastors." Never mind that their new churches were small. They had run out of patience with normal kid behavior, and it was time to step up to the heady heights of *real* ministry.

You might be thinking, "Not me, never!" You're not fired, you're fired up! You have every intention of being a great youth worker. You're enthused and pumped. You're excited about seeing young people come to Christ, being discipled in him, and being unleashed to impact their campuses for God. You want to stay in youth ministry a long time. Or, even if you're not a "lifer," you're going to do an excellent job until the time comes for you to do something else.

Youth workers feel excited, awed, and optimistic about the ministry years ahead. Happily, many actually see their ministry dreams come true. The sad fact is, though, that many don't. Actually, the odds are against you. Most don't make it past five years without getting fired or resigning in disillusionment. I have been in youth ministry over two decades and know that some of those who played "Risk" with me this year won't be around next.

Why? Why is it that some make it in youth work and others don't? That's what this book is about. We're going to look together at the reasons men and women who start out so enthusiastically in youth ministry eventually resign in despair. We'll see why so many who start out fired up end up getting fired instead. I have researched nearly 200 cases in which youth pastors have lost their jobs. Some saw it coming, others got surprised, but they all were fired. Consequently, we're going to take a hard look at the issues of conflict, competency, and compromise that so often prove toxic to a youth worker who lasts even a couple of years. And for those who've already had a broken world experience in youth ministry, we'll take a look at how to begin to put it back together again.

This book is meant to both equip and encourage. Equipping is appropriate because none of us is perfect. Encouragement is good because when the kids are apathetic, the parents complain, and our pastor seems aloof, it's hard not to wonder if we shouldn't have gone into farming, Amway, or real estate after all.

As I write this, I am celebrating my thirteenth year as youth pastor of the church in Seattle, where I now serve. Believe me, it hasn't been easy. In that amount of time, I have had three senior pastors resign and one die. I have, of necessity, become an expert at interim solutions. I have seen the money situation at the church so tight that we couldn't afford to mail the letters that would inform the congregation we had a big problem.

I nearly resigned after three and a half years. After that long, I couldn't blame the problems in the youth ministry on my predecessor. The kids were basically selfish and it really annoyed me. Youth group numbers weren't increasing and that hurt my self-image. Worst of all, I didn't know what to do next.

Being at my previous church three years, doing short-term youth ministry while in seminary before that, and serving three years in a church while attending a university before that, had set my internal body clock to get restless at three-year intervals. Having not been anywhere longer than this, I literally did not know what to do in year four.

I had some offers to go elsewhere. I chose to stay and see for myself what would happen next. More than ten years have passed since then! It is worth it to stay. It is worth the effort, time, and struggle. I consider any stay of five years or more to be "long-term," and here are some reasons why it's worth it to have five years as a goal.

ELEVEN PAYOFFS FOR LONG-TERM YOUTH MINISTRY

1. Increased Credibility. Kids aren't stupid. If the leadership pattern for them has been a revolving door of nine- to twelve-month youth leaders, the kids are going to be reluctant to open up to us. As the months turn into years, though, they will see our obvious commitment and our obvious care.

In my fourth year at North Seattle Alliance Church, I took the youth group Christmas caroling on "porno row" in downtown Seattle. The kids, and their parents, were a little skeptical, but they listened to my reasons for wanting to do this and agreed. No way could I have pulled that off after only six months as youth pastor!

Assuming we're not totally incompetent, our credibility with parents increases as well, the longer we stay. When I graduated from seminary at age twenty-five, I thought of myself as an adult and I expected to be respected as one. No such luck! Many parents viewed me as just an older kid. Credibility began to come, though, as I stayed put. It also helped when my wife and I had children of our own. Then the parents really began to believe that I was capable of understanding a parent's point of view.

2. The Joy of Watching Young People Grow Up. It really is amazing to watch them grow! Think of it . . . at twelve years old they come in skinny, awkward, and shy. What a change in the next five or six years! Our church honors the high school graduates every June. As I serve them communion, my mind runs instant replays of all the personal memories of retreats, lunches, crises, despair, and laughter we shared together.

3. Lower Stress. The longer we stay in youth ministry, the more experience we get at handling tough times. Take a few laps around the calendar track and youth ministry "biggies"—like retreats, conventions, and major programs—don't seem so overwhelming.

When it comes to personal disasters, very little comes as a surprise any more. I have just about seen it all . . . a leadership team member got pregnant, a sixteen-year-old left town with (and married) her Sunday school teacher, and my life was threatened. I had to advise a seventeen-year-old who was leading a big program what to do if disgruntled parishioners (who had already threatened to picket the event) tried to storm the stage and grab the microphone. Crises like suicide attempts, hate mail, fatal accidents, kids in jail . . . these things tend to be overwhelming at first.

But you know, it's not quite such a crisis the second or third time around. True, these things are never fun, but when we experience them, it prepares us for the next time. I've seen the dark side of the Christian church. I've seen the underside of people's souls. By the amount of human wreckage that washes up at my office door as a pastor, I recognize we're in a spiritual battle. That high tide of pain can wash me away and out of ministry, or it can, by God's grace, strengthen me to serve him better. The longer we stay in youth ministry, the longer our backlog of badness. Experience serves to make us steadier and stronger when the next tragedy or crisis hits.

4. Control Over Schedule. The more experienced we get at planning and massaging the yearly schedule, the easier it gets to do so with our own sanity and our family's feelings in mind.

5. Youth Ministry Keeps Us Young. This isn't a big concern if we're twenty-two, but past thirty it does become an issue. I'm appalled at how old some of my chronological peers seem. For some, getting older means getting closed minded, rigid, and physically unhealthy. We can't stay in youth ministry without being open, flexible, and growing as a person. Being with teenagers certainly helps us to keep growing and learning in our personal lives.

6. Stay and It May Begin to Pay. We're not in it for the money, right? Yet it does not hurt to receive a wage that helps us put a roof over our head, raise a family, give cheerfully to the Lord's work, and put a little money aside for the future. More and more churches are realizing that long-haul youth ministry people are valuable, rare, and worth the price to keep.

7. Spiritual Impact. Seventh in this list, but not seventh in importance, of course, is the eventual worldwide impact of our youth ministry. Staying at least five years will mean we get to see some of the long-term fruit. If we provide a positive role model of what it means to be in Christian service, some will sense God's leading in the same direction. Some of those kids will want to be missionaries, youth pastors, or other "full-time" workers. It is very exciting to see those who graduate from our youth group get involved in ministry themselves. It is 2 Timothy 2:2 in actual practice!

8. Partializing Big Tasks. When I came to North Seattle Alliance Church, I had a vision in mind. I was also aware of the huge amount of restructuring needed to make it happen. It was comforting to know I did not have to do it all in the first year. My first year, we really focused on getting people involved in discipleship training. Year two saw the complete revamping of Sunday school and the beginning of an intern training program. The third year I focused intensely on upgrading our volunteer staff. Year four I began, with much fanfare, a "Project Ministries" program. This was to be a service-oriented ministry, where kids would select from six social action options. It failed so spectacularly that it took two more years to clean up the mess and get the totally revised program started under a different name.

The point is, if we're planning on a long stay, we've got time. Short of the Second Coming, we've got the time to patiently work our plans and repair the damages when they fail. I still think that way; each year I tinker with the ministry a little more and try new things. There's plenty of time.

9. The Joy of Being Good at Something. It's fun to do something well, and to sense God's affirmation of his gifts in us in ministry. If we have a long-haul perspective, we learn to shore up our weaknesses and capitalize on our strengths. I'm not a good counselor; musically I am laughably ignorant; I have no high-profile collegiate or professional sports career in my past; and speaking at a retreat makes me tremble in fear. But I do know how to create a positive atmosphere in a group of kids. I do know how to motivate kids to deepen their walks with God. I'm a good planner and a good "people resource" manager. I love to organize things and then watch other people be up front.

It's a good feeling to be good at a few things, and to have the chance to use the strengths God has given me.

10. The Joy of Watching Problem People Graduate Out of My Life. No individual youth worker can relate equally well to everyone or please everyone. I am no exception. Some kids in the youth group don't care much for me or the ministry we've built. They are occasionally critical, but I try my best to reconcile and build bridges of friendship. Sometimes, though, it is just not possible. So what do I do then? I give up! No, I don't quit praying for them, and I am still cordial. Yet the time comes when I quit spending emotional energy on them.

Sooner or later the happy day comes . . . they graduate!

It's not hard to tell when they don't like you. Near the end of their freshman year, Jill and her three friends held their own "class" in the women's washroom on Sunday mornings . . . apparently with the blessing of their parents. If they knew I was going to be out of town, they might emerge from their water closet sanctuary and attend. And so it went for three long years . . . and graduation Sunday was a happy day for all of us. Jill is married now and lives out of state. About once a year she visits home and is in church. When I see her, I have an almost irresistible urge to go to the washroom.

Think of it . . . when it comes to problem people, a senior pastor has no such graduation day to look forward to. The senior pastor has to wait until problem people either leave or die. It may be a looonnng wait, too. Youth workers seldom have to wait longer than five years.

11. Things Get Easier and Take Less Time. Bible studies, Sunday school lessons, and retreats used to take hours, if not days, to get ready for. If we stay longer than a couple of years, the ministry basics become easier as we get a better feel for what works and what doesn't.

Our high school group is on a four-year curriculum rotation for both Sunday morning and Wednesday nights (see Appendix C). I wrote much of the Sunday morning material myself. I had the time to do this because other aspects of the ministry took less time to pull off. Stay longer than five years, and the payoffs are even greater. The Bible book our senior high group is due to look at this spring is 1 and 2 Peter. I'll pull all my preparation notes from four years ago.

I'll completely revamp some of the studies. I'll use most of them just as they are.

Similarly, big retreats are no big deal to prepare for. Because we save everything (notes, schedules, publicity brochures, confirmation letters to speakers, names of musicians, and camp facilities), we don't have to reinvent the floppy disk every time we sit down at the computer. Last summer we had the best attended and finest retreat our high school group has ever had. Aside from prayer, my preparation time was less than three hours *total*. In the early days, that same retreat would have taken twenty-five hours.

* * *

You're fired up, you want to last, and you're willing to work to make it happen. Your excitement is high and so are your goals. You don't want to become a statistic on some denominational tally sheet. You want to avoid becoming a ministry casualty. Let's look first at why good and sincere youth workers get disillusioned. Why do well-intentioned and once enthusiastic men and women bail out of youth work? There are many reasons.

CHAPTER TWO

MOVING IN, MOVING UP, MOVING OUT

THE VALLEY OF THE SHADOW: THE "MORALE CURVE TROUGH"

From the world of business comes a slice of truth that we experience when we start a new ministry. It could be our first ministry, or it could be our zillionth. Virtually everyone who goes to a new job cycles through a predictable range of feelings.[1] Some bail out at the bottom, or trough, of the morale curve, just three to six months after arriving.

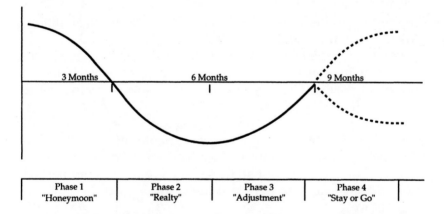

Phase One: The Honeymoon. We land in our first ministry position with much enthusiasm and optimism. Kids are happy to see us; parents are grateful we've come. We feel good about our new church and its senior pastor. Everything, or at least nearly everything, looks great. It's why we've come. We're ready to roll. Our adrenaline is pumping as we launch.

Phase Two: Reality Sets In. "You mean the youth group has always staffed children's church and that means I'm in charge of that, too? Why didn't anyone bother to tell me this before?"

"Gosh, I really miss going to the lake with my friends back home."

"I thought I was poverty-stricken as a student. Now I'm a youth pastor and I'm *really* poor."

"I'm going to be out six nights a week, *every* week?"

No matter how wonderful our new place of ministry, some aspects of the place and the job will not be exactly as we envisioned. If we had close ties with our previous church, we feel the loss deeply. We miss the people and places we called home. Like peeling back layers of wallpaper in an old fixer home, we learn more and more what the new job really entails and what is expected of us. For many, the worst feelings of discouragement come four to six months after arriving.

Phase Three: Adjustment Attempts. Some youth workers resign after just a few months. The weight of reality is more than they can shoulder. Time to feel a calling to a different situation. Most of us, however, carry on. At least we do for a while.

Now that we really understand that our pastor is not very supportive, the parents tend to gripe, we can't afford to live in a nice apartment, and children's chapels plus daily Vacation Bible School is unalterably on our job description, we try to adjust. One-by-one we come to terms with the negatives. Can we live with them? Can we change them? Are we capable of doing this? We take the realities we now see and compare them with the resources we have. We put all these ingredients into our mental stew and stir. Then we decide if the result is palatable. Which brings us to. . . .

Phase Four: Stay and Grow or Exit. This decision point comes in nine to twelve months. Do we stay and try to work things out? Do we head for the copy shop to print an updated resume? Even if we survive the "morale curve trough," we may get to Phase Four and conclude it's just not worth the hassle to stay.

We experience the morale curve not only when we move to a new job, but also when our job description changes.

Though we cannot do much about the morale curve, we can do a lot about how high the highs are and how low the lows are. The highs and the lows depend on how much accurate information about our jobs we get in advance of coming. The clearer our picture in advance, the more we'll understand the negatives when we arrive. We thus do not have as far to fall in Phase Two because our honeymoon at Phase One wasn't so high. The more realistic our appraisal, the easier it is to adjust (Phase Three) and move ahead (Phase Four) because we've foreseen these problems in the first place.

It also is comforting just to realize that this progression of feelings and experiences is absolutely normal. Getting into Phase Four and choosing to stay can result in increasing effectiveness as we do the work of our ministry.

IDEALISM:
BAMBI VERSUS GODZILLA

We come into youth ministry fresh, innocent, idealistic, and so sincere. We romp through the morale curve trough undaunted and proceed toward the high meadows. We believe that this is the way it will always be. We may be too starry-eyed and distracted to hear the thudding footsteps of some monster issue or crisis. Then. . . splat. We are crushed by the facts and realities in our own youth ministry. This collision of reality and idealism sends some youth workers packing . . . choosing to find a better place or a better line of work. What are some of these "godzillas of reality" ?

1. How Christian People Should Act. We work in the church, right? Full of Christians, right? People who believe in grace and forgiveness; people who want to live the fruit of the Spirit, right? Don't count on it.

"Len, you've been here five months and I'm convinced your true purpose is to destroy this youth group and all that Matt tried to build."

It was my first church after seminary. This was said loudly, with anger, and in front of ten young people, in the middle of what was supposed to be a nice social. Guess what? I didn't sleep very well that night.

"Len, in this notebook we've written down all the mistakes we feel you've made in the last several years. If we don't get what we want from you tonight, we will make what is in here public."

A marriage in the youth staff had blown apart. Another staffer was charged with causing the breakup. Everyone had chosen sides. Some had decided it was all my fault.

We have in our minds that Christians should act like Christians in the church. The reality is that sometimes they don't, and woe be to us if we get in harm's way.

I'm no psychologist, but I know that people deal with grief in different ways. The grief could be about any sort of loss—a death in the family, a divorce, a change in the program; it doesn't much matter. Some people deal with grief by getting stuck at the angry stage. They need someone to kick, someone to destroy, someone to ruin. More than once, I have been the unfortunate recipient of a crusade of terror and it's been a nightmare from hell itself. Ever wondered if your wife and children should sit at different locations in the church so a gunman couldn't kill them all? Believe me, it's a little distracting.

2. What the Ministry Should Be Like. We might envision that youth ministry will be a glorious series of revivals, leading kids to Christ, counseling with them, and guiding them spiritually. Any youth pastor who's been around a while will affirm that youth ministry, properly done, involves an immense amount of desk work and administration. Youth workers are not famous for their love of administration.

From our youth ministry desk, we ponder the whole church and expect that people will be eager to see changes that will help accomplish the mission of reaching and discipling people for Christ. Are you in a church like that? Praise God. The rest of us must subsist on crumbs of progress rationed out sparingly by church boards and committees.

We have the idea that things should be fair, too. Senior pastors and church boards should deal fairly with problems and issues. Thank God if you've never seen unfairness in the church!

3. Our Own Authority. We're called to lead, to innovate, to inspire—right? As youth pastors, we each expect to be respected as a leader. That Bambi-type idealism is easily crushed. If we're under thirty, and especially if we don't have any kids of our own, many adults will give us respect that is only slightly above that which they give to a fourteen-year-old. Our decisions can be undermined, our motives questioned.

4. The Youths Themselves. We expect kids to be hungry for God as we teach and lead them. We expect that they'll like our ideas and have a deep commitment to the Lord and the youth group.

Although some kids are radically committed to Christ, the sad fact is, most aren't. Greg doesn't come to our Bible studies so he can grow deep in the Word of God; he comes so he can sit by Ellen. Marlene doesn't come to our Friday night social happy about reaching out to new kids and helping shy ones feel included; she's excited because her parents are away for the weekend and two of her friends from the group are coming over to spend the night after the event. She's *very* excited because she's rented three R-rated movies. Not violent movies, of course ("Why do boys like that stuff, anyway?"). There will be lots of romance, though, lots of skin, and lots of sex. Marlene's still a virgin, but that's a stigma she hopes to shed soon.

It can be a real blow when we realize just how carnal, how pagan, and how totally seduced by the world many of our kids are. We may find it very hard to love kids who live way below what we expect of them. Without love, we'll soon find an excuse to leave.

Speaking of youths, we also idealize that as the months and years go by, more of them will join the youth group because of our wonderful ministry. I sure felt this way. I got a heavy dose of reality when my statistics showed youth group growth *and* decline tracked solidly with Sunday morning worship attendance.

CHANGING HEARTS, CHANGING BODIES

We may start out strong in youth ministry, but then our passion for youth fades. Our own maturation can mean working with youth becomes more and more like a cross-cultural ministry. This internal rewiring of passion and preferences means many leave youth ministry for the pulpit or other adult ministries.

Physically, it's easy to go downhill in a hurry past thirty. If there's always something better to do than to get regular exercise, and if there's always another day to start eating right, we won't get far into the thirties before our bodies resemble the contours of apples or pears. It's a rare apple and it's a rare pear that can maintain the energy level that good youth ministry requires.

SO SAD

It was a cool and rainy mid-November Saturday morning. As usual, I had looked forward to the monthly Junior High Cabinet meeting. I had always believed that junior high school kids are much more capable of spiritual growth and leadership than people give them credit for, and this group of spiritually motivated and ministry-minded kids was a good case in point.

We had made breakfast together in the church kitchen and now it was time to settle down. On the agenda was the happy business of prayer and planning the group activities. September and October had gone very well, and great events were on the calendar for us to look forward to. In the two years I'd been at the church, the junior high ministry had become famous for the right reasons.

"So, before we start planning, how do you feel it's going in the group these days?" I asked.

Jana began. "I think its going terrible. Shella, that new girl, is so obnoxious."

"Yeah, I agree," answered Charlie. "None of the events are any fun any more."

"I don't even look forward to coming," added Karen.

"I don't like it either, and I think my family might start looking for a different church," Ron added helpfully.

Believe or not, the conversation went downhill from there. Negativism was expressed with vehemence and bitter conviction. For me, it was an agonizing hour. When they seemed to be done I asked, "Does anyone have anything positive, anything good about the group, they want to say?"

Seven pairs of eyes looked back at me. No one responded, not even one. I was so totally blown away that all I could do was close with a brief prayer. After spending the next hour taking all of them home in the church van, I went back to my office and sat at my desk, lost in thought. Damage control time. If this had been my first ministry, no doubt I would have composed a resignation letter. I decided instead to do nothing unusual. Why?

"Len, you stupid jerk," I kindly said to myself, "you forgot it was November."

November . . . it's one of the four reasons youth workers get discouraged and quit.

Seasonal Affective Disorder (SAD) . . . that's the fancy clinical name. In my first few years of ministry I didn't know the clinical name for it, but I did notice a distinct pattern. What I noticed then and still notice today is that some of our brightest and best will go into a spiritual tailspin in November. They'll get negative and critical . . . the fire in their words seems like it is straight from hell. Some young people will get this way and so will some adults.

I used to lie awake at night thinking about this . . . worrying, praying, wondering why. I tried to use counseling or "heavy" talks with the group or individuals as early weapons. It only took a few years to figure out, however, that no amount of prayer, counseling, and extra meetings would make any difference. All I had to do was wait . . . by mid or late December, the grumpy kids and adults would snap out of it and be their cheerful and positive selves again.

Seasonal Affective Disorder is very well documented. The *Journal of the American Medical Association* and *Scientific American* have both discussed it recently.[2] It's in the popular press, too: *USA Today, Sports Illustrated, Business Horizons*, and even *Vogue* among many others. Some people show signs of SAD in May, too. My term for that is "The May-November Blahs," but the researchers call it "Summer SAD."

SAD exists because of the change to and from daylight savings time that we all experience twice a year; this change causes a fluctuation in the amount of daily light we see. The time change is also coupled with worse weather or better weather, and less sunshine or more sunshine. This change of light level affects the body's production of a chemical called *melatonin*. In some people, this change in melatonin level produces symptoms of depression. In other words, people get grumpy. Six weeks is about what it takes to readjust, though some people have the symptoms through all the winter months.

Youth workers who don't know about this are doubly vulnerable. We are vulnerable first because we're clueless as to why we get blindsided by people who we thought were on our side. Nice, friendly, supportive people all of a sudden want to see our ministries filleted and our souls hung on meat hooks . . . fodder for the circling vultures they and others have become.

Second, we are vulnerable because we ourselves may be victims of SAD. Things might be going okay and then, without apparent cause or warning, our internal "self-talk" gets negative. We internally rehearse long, critical speeches to kids, board members, or our senior pastor. We compose our resignation letters, dream of how nice it would be to be to change churches, and speculate on how unjust it is that someone so wonderful as we could be stuck with such ungrateful people.

If we live in Florida or Southern California, chances are we may have never seen SAD. One study showed that the farther north a person went in North America, the greater the percentage of people who were *severely* affected.[3]

Florida	1.4 percent
Maryland	6.3 percent
New York	8.0 percent
New Hampshire	10.0 percent

These percentages represent the severe cases. An equal percentage of SAD sufferers will experience only moderate symptoms. What does it mean? If we live in Baltimore, St. Louis, Denver, or Eureka, and we minister to fifty junior and senior high school kids, about seven or eight will experience the significant emotional undertow of SAD. It's only a small number, but the destructive potential is frightening.

Knowing this, what do I do about SAD? (1) Every November I remind the youth group and volunteer staff about SAD. I tell them that the feelings, if they come, are normal. I implore them not to drop out during this time, but to be around people who can encourage them. (2) Personally, I have a policy to never, ever, resign from *anything* in November. (3) When I go to youth pastor meetings, I try to watch for those who are feeling low and encourage them, if I can.

ANY SOLUTIONS?

In this chapter, we have toured the reasons many youth workers choose to get off the bus. Are there any easy solutions to these issues? Actually, there are!

1. Being Aware. It sounds almost too simple, but just knowing about SAD will help. Unaware of SAD and the morale curve trough? Now you *are* aware.

Jim moved from San Diego to Portland, Oregon, when he came to work at his new church. He'd read about SAD and he knew there were a lot of niceties about life in San Diego he would miss dearly. He began his ministry July first and sure enough, in mid-November, he was feeling the pull toward home. He put a big picture of the ocean up in his office, and he shared his feelings openly with the pastoral staff and other youth pastors he saw frequently. He made it through his first winter and now, three years later, he's an avid backpacker. He loves Portland and loves how close the mountains are. The ocean picture in his office has been replaced by one of Mt. Hood.

2. Being Real. Having our ideals crushed by reality is never fun. Youth workers who survive the shattering of early ideals do so largely because they truly love young people, they deeply feel a call from God to be in youth ministry, and they have a support network.

Cindy went to her second church assuming her senior pastor would be warm, supportive, and caring. Her first senior pastor had been that way. Surprise! Her new pastor was aloof and never talked at a feeling level; soon Cindy felt like she'd made a big mistake. She almost resigned the day after he told her, "Look, I don't need or want to be your friend, get that through your head." Cindy got active with a support group for youth pastors that met monthly. She found several other youth ministers had pastors like that. She successfully let go of her expectations about her pastor and this group began to meet her needs for caring support.

We'll consider these survival necessities again in Chapters Seven and Fourteen.

3. Being Honest. There is nothing wrong with changing our minds. We may have set out with high hopes of long-term ministry with kids, but now our changing hearts pull us in a different direction. It's okay. In fact, it's better to leave than to stay for the wrong reasons. More on this in Chapter Thirteen.

4. Being Centered. The surest way to survive discouragement and setback in the early years of ministry is to remain centered on Jesus Christ. He is our comfort when we hurt, our security when our surroundings shake. The apostle Paul certainly had his share of bad days and setbacks: "We are hard pressed on every side, but not crushed; perplexed, but not in despair; persecuted, but not abandoned; struck down, but not destroyed. . . . we do not lose heart. Though outwardly we are wasting away, yet inwardly we are being renewed day by day. For our light and momentary troubles are achieving for us an eternal glory that far outweighs them all" (2 Corinthians 4:8, 9, 16, 17).

Yes, sometimes it seems like we must slog through the slime to be youth pastors. Yet, when we are properly centered on our relationship with Christ, we can keep from being swallowed up.

* * *

We see that some youth workers who start strong eventually make their own choice to change churches or change careers. Unfortunately, others have the choice made for them. They get fired. Some may see it coming. Others are surprised. In both cases, it's no fun.

We're now going to look at the additional hazards of the first few years of ministry. Of those who get fired, it happens to 50 percent of them in *just the first two years.* Why? Is it sex and scandal? Hardly. Moral compromise is one of the least likely causes for the ax to fall. If not sex, what? We'll now look at the three "C's," and we'll take it from the top.

CHAPTER THREE

CAUTION:
CONFLICT COMING

I held the envelope in my hand for a few moments before tearing it open. Seeing the return address, I knew the nature of what was inside.

"Dear Pastor Kageler,
"With regards to your so-called youth rally next month, I am writing to inform you again that I feel what you have planned is a godless abomination. I am writing our headquarters and our Christian college presidents, as well as the other pastors in our district to ask them to join me in fasting and prayer, and to call upon God to stop this evil. You will be held accountable by almighty God for the deception and worldliness you are fostering among our precious young people.
"I intend to do everything in my power to stop this event. . . ."

Conflict (v. or n.) kon'flikt 1. to come into collision; 2. to contend; do battle. n. 3. a battle or struggle, esp. a prolonged struggle.[1]
That is how the dictionary describes it. *Collision . . . battle, struggle . . .* these are the words that define it. What are the feelings that define it? Try these: shock, betrayal, confusion, hopelessness, doubting, anger, and uncertainty. Conflict is the first of the three "Big C's" and 95 percent of youth pastors who get fired name some kind of conflict as the reason. If we think we can be in youth ministry and avoid conflict, we are fooling ourselves. Conflict may not result in our getting fired, but it's sure to come our way at some point in our first few years of ministry. It's a major ministry hazard.

With the unanimous support of our elders, the youth rally went ahead as planned. It was clear to many who attended that the Lord was powerfully present that night. Wow, with so much prayer from all over the country, how could it have been otherwise?

In any conflict it takes two to tango. Of those who get fired in youth ministry, here is who they name as their tango partners (the people with whom they have collided):

1. Senior pastors   42 percent
2. Church boards   27 percent
3. Parents   18 percent
4. Kids   9 percent

If we want to last in ministry, we must learn to work successfully with these four groups of people. In Chapters Five through Seven we will consider the positive skills needed to do so. Here, let's first just try to understand what the issues are. Let's start with the single biggest source of youth pastor stomach upset . . . the senior pastor.

THE SENIOR PASTOR: FRIEND OR FOE?

There are at least four factors that cause conflict between the youth pastor and the senior pastor. Let's listen to some of the respondents to my survey of "fired" youth pastors.

1. Differing Philosophies of Ministry.

> *"Two weeks after arriving at a new youth work job, the founding senior pastor, who had raised the congregation to be one of the largest in the denomination, died of a heart attack. Several months later, I sat in the study of my new senior pastor to discuss my dreams for the youth ministry. I was obviously enthusiastic about building a team that could generate deep and lasting relationships with the church's teenagers. In fact, I was in the process of building such relationships, I continued, and the youths seemed to be responding. . . .*
>
> *"At this point the pastor straightened up in his chair, looked at me across his acre of desk, and said, 'If you're going to succeed in a church this size, you can't expect to get too close to the students. You'll*

have to keep your distance. This isn't a small opera-
tion, you know.'
". . . In a very short time it became clear to me that
my approach to ministry was out of sync with his."[2]

This conflict didn't result in termination. The youth pastor hung on for a couple of years and then found another position. It's a perfect example of a philosophy of ministry conflict. The pastor wanted a more managerial approach to ministry, while the youth worker believed in a more relational style. It's very easy to get fired over a difference in ministry philosophies. My survey revealed many such cases.

"I got fired because my heart and soul were dedicat-
ed to winning unchurched kids to Christ. He wanted
my emphasis to be 99 percent on kids who were
already churched."

"I thought the denominational curriculum was sick.
He told me to use it or else. I didn't. I got fired."

2. Pastoral Insecurity. Woe be to the youth pastor who has a boss with a poor self-image. Success in the youth ministry, especially if it's numerical growth, can cause a senior pastor to get uneasy. The congregation might see the youth pastor as a much better communicator than the senior pastor. Here is such a story from my file of firings, this one from Canada.

"The youth pastor was very intelligent and articulate.
He was also warm and very committed to God and
to being true before him. He was an excellent leader.
So when he saw the church was dying fast, he was
concerned and shared some ideas with the senior
pastor. The pastor took this as rejection and criti-
cism. He had the church leadership fire the youth
pastor."

3. Scapegoat. It makes us mad. It's not fair. We may even wonder if God exists after seeing it happen or having it happen to us. I am not, by nature, an angry person, but scapegoat firings really tick me off.

> *"I had been the youth pastor for ten years. The church had grown in the past and had continued to grow under our new senior pastor. A few of the parents and people of the church were unhappy because we listened to contemporary Christian music in the youth group. These people put a lot of pressure on him. He chose to fire me instead of support me. He thought it would be easier to get a new youth pastor than to get these people to shut up. I was devastated. Well, at least they gave me six months severance pay."*

Does that make you mad? Good.

4. New Pastor Equals New Staff. Some churches require that when a senior pastor resigns, the whole pastoral staff must resign, too. This gives the new pastor the ability to bring in his or her own team. In churches that don't automatically take this approach, a new senior pastor might still maneuver to get the others out.

> *"Our new pastor told me that the church could no longer afford to pay my salary and that therefore I was terminated. I could take my time finding a new position, but it only took me a couple of months. I was glad to get out of there. Four weeks later they hired a new youth pastor at the same salary I was receiving. The new youth pastor was the son of my new pastor's best friend. Needless to say, it makes me cynical about the politics and power plays that take place in the church."*

Speaking of politics and power plays. . . .

CHURCH BOARDS: WHEN IN DOUBT, BLAME IT ON THE YOUTH PASTOR

If we find ourselves in a church that has supportive, visionary, and positive lay leadership, we should drop to our knees daily and thank God. Churches with leadership like that do exist. Unfortunately, we can't just assume that people get into church leadership because of their spiritual qualifications, vision, and insight. When we head into a new church situation, we can't assume the church board will be a source of blessing and will support us.

Conflicts with church boards often mirror those the senior pastor has with us. It is not hard for him to rally leadership at this level to support his cause. In addition, problems with church boards often have to do with issues of property and program. Here are a few comments I've heard or heard about over the years.

> *"The young people have no respect for the church bus. When they're done, it looks like a pig pen."*

> *"They had no right to paint the youth room without consulting the deacons first!"*

> *"Patsy, do you realize that after your program last night the janitor found cigarette ashes in the main bathroom?"*

> *"I don't like the dancing the youth choir does when they sing."*

> *"Why are you having a pudding fight when there are millions of people starving in Africa?"*

> *"There's not enough Bible teaching in Sunday school. When I was that age, we had a sixty-minute Bible study every Sunday and we really learned something."*

PARENTS:
THEY'LL LOVE YA OR HATE YA

Parents have a vested interest in youth ministry because they entrust their daughters and sons to us each week. If we fail to grasp the parents' point of view very early in our ministry, we guarantee conflict at best and dismissal at worst. Nearly one in five youth pastors who get the ax name conflict with parents as the cause. Over what kinds of issues do youth pastors and parents often collide?

Rules, Standards, and Control. When we enter youth ministry, our first priority is building good rapport with the kids themselves. We want to be seen as nice people. We want to be liked. Churched junior and senior highers aren't stupid . . . they know we want them to like us. In fact, *they know our job depends on them*. This can give them a sense of power over us. They know we'll be more lenient with them than their parents are, and some will get maximum mileage out of this situation.

Retreats, lock-ins, and other overnighters . . . these are all essential items on the youth ministry program menu. We hold these events because they offer the greatest opportunity for ministry. They also offer the greatest opportunity for disaster.

Junior high school kids love to stay up all night. When an all-nighter or a retreat is over, we say goodbye to them in the church parking lot and go home to take a nap. Parents, on the other hand, have to suffer with these sleep-deprived terrors until they are rested enough to be civil again. Our credibility falls when we end the event with kids who are zombies or gremlins.

Most parents prefer that their kids come back from events alive and unmaimed. Serendipitous cliff diving, drag racing with the church bus, and other acts of macho heroism will all be lauded by the kids. Rest assured, however, they'll come home and expand the truth to tell an even more exciting story. Rest assured, also, that this will not play well with the parents.

Carl, a new youth worker with junior highers, thought he'd give the kids a little thrill while heading home from the camping weekend. On a mountain road, with a drop-off on one side, he accelerated when he saw the "Caution, Dip, 10 MPH" sign. The dip was actually a washout—five feet steeply down, twenty-five feet level, and five feet steeply up. Behaving more like an F16 fighter pilot than a bus driver, he hit the washout at 35 MPH. Those in the back of the bus were thrown from their seats nearly to the ceiling. Those who had been napping found themselves on the floor. Suitcases and sleeping bags rained from the luggage racks. Kids roared with approval, chaperones (having just aged a decade) silently thanked God they were still alive, and John beamed in acknowledgement of his oh-so-cool machoness.

It was all pretty funny until the pastor's phone started to light up the next day as parents called registering their dismay.

Funny thing, parents also prefer that their kids not be given opportunities to become sexually active on youth group outings.

My heart sank the day after a backpacking trip when I heard the news that a bunch of kids had shared tents and sleeping bags the last night of the trip. I heard this news from an angry parent. A medical emergency had resulted in one of our three hiking groups being left without adult supervision for one night. I assumed that after the worship services they, being aware of the long and hard hike out ahead the next day, would go to bed and get a good night's sleep. Well, they went to bed all right.

Back on the home front, if anarchy rules the Sunday school classroom, the parents will know. Not only will they know, but they'll question why we're letting it happen. I know of at least two cases where "lack of control" was the main reason the parents crusaded for the youth pastor's removal.

Teaching and Advice. Some parents care, and care very deeply, about our counsel and teaching. They'll quiz their sons and daughters about what we teach in class and about what we discuss during personal visits.

"Pastor Kageler, did you really tell my daughter to keep dating Chris, even though we don't approve?"

"Well, er, ah . . ." my mind replayed (at triple speed) my conversation with Sandy the day before. This particular parent, for whatever reason, had always seemed unhappy with me. Fortunately, my stock went back up to zero as I assured her I would call Sandy within twenty-four hours and clarify that she must have misunderstood something I had said.

It is important to think through any counsel we give kids. It is especially important when the issue is parent/teen relations. If we are in an evangelical church, our teaching better have some solid Biblical foundation.

> *"We fired Fred because he was off base and unbalanced in his teaching. He was always into prophecy . . . setting dates, identifying world leaders with specific scriptures . . . that sort of thing. We talked to him about it, but it just got worse and worse. Then he became convinced that the world would end on a certain week when all the planets were lined up in a certain way. He told the young people they shouldn't bother going to school, just stay home and pray. He stayed home, too . . . didn't show at the office all week. Well, the world didn't end, but Fred's job did. There's more. His wife left him a few weeks later . . . guess it's hard living with a prophet."*

KIDS: ON YOUR SIDE UNTIL . . .

Yes, we can expect some conflict here, too. Nine percent of youth pastors who have been fired name conflict with kids as a reason. Many more of us, however, experience verbal or volitional collisions with kids at least occasionally. There are four areas to watch out for.

1. Not Being Like Our Predecessor. When we begin a new ministry, it is normal that we take someone's place. The old youth pastor has left, and we're the new kid on the block. Change is hard for young people in the youth group. If they liked the last youth leader, we're guaranteed conflict if we're very different. Furthermore, if they nearly worshiped our predecessor, figure most of the current ninth through twelfth graders are a lost cause. Focus on the seventh and eighth graders . . . they don't have so many cherished memories. I learned this the hard way in my first church after seminary.

My predecessor's name was Matt. The young people had nearly deified him. Matt was a seventy-five-hour-a-week youth pastor. He was *always* with them . . . always available for a pickup game of basketball or volleyball. On Thanksgiving and Christmas afternoons he was at the church gym with the kids. His first kid was born while he was on a youth event. This guy ate, drank, slept, and breathed youth ministry. His wife apparently didn't mind. The church board asked him to not work so much, but Matt paid no attention.

I began my ministry there seven days after his farewell service, and three days after the youth group had tearfully helped him load the moving van. Unfortunately for me, I was a fifty-five-hour-a-week youth man, not seventy-five.

For eighteen long months, it seemed like every day I heard "Matt this" and "Matt that." Seeking to avoid pain, I naturally gravitated toward the junior high school kids. They had liked him too, but at least he wasn't God. I found special comfort with nerdy seventh grade boys . . . I felt like a nerd, too. My breakthrough came when we did a junior high musical that the whole church thought was a "ten." In my last eighteen months there, even the older kids figured out how much I loved them, and they let me express it in my own ways.

My farewell service was a tearjerker, and we cried again while loading the moving van. Kurt came after me and eighteen months later *he* was finally out of *my* shadow. And that's about how long it takes to win the hearts of kids who dearly love someone else.

2. Changing Cherished Programs. We have our plans and programs in youth ministry. In our first few years, we'll no doubt change a program, a structure, a way something is done.

If we are unlucky enough to be in a group that needs dividing . . . junior high from senior high, or senior high from college . . . watch out: Conflict is coming. Boards may agree the change is necessary, parents may be all for it, but watch out because *one* group of people will fight us all the way. Maybe it will be the girls—not all girls, but girls just below the cutoff line. Eighth grade girls will fight to stay with the ninth to twelfth graders and twelfth grade girls will kill to remain with college kids.

Are the kids so ministry minded they resent a narrowing of their mission field? Not exactly. Yes, they come unglued because their field is narrowing . . . but it's the males they're worried about. Eighth grade girls aspire to eleventh grade boys, not thirteen-year-olds. Sweet seventeens lose little sleep about their chronological peers, but dream on about college men or even postcollege men.

3. Rules and Regulations. Valiantly we attempt to please parents and pastors by exorcising anarchy in the classroom, youth programs, and retreats. In doing so, we win the respect of most kids, too. But not all.

According to James Dobson, 21.1 percent of those in our youth group will be *very* strong willed and another 13.3 percent *rather* strong willed.[3] Among these will be a good number of kids who are second born among the children in their families. These kids tend to have rebel tendencies, are heavily influenced by peer pressure, and like to push authorities to the limit.[4]

Strong-willed kids enjoy hearing our rules and expectations like cats enjoy having fur stroked backwards. Inside, their spirits arch. Outside, they may choose to be passive, but their body language will scream defiance. If they're not passive, we'll notice—no doubt about it. We can expect this as we begin our first months and years of ministry in a new location . . . the strong-willed ones will find ways to test our limits and gauge our reactions. This may bring us into conflict, or, if handled well, it may not.

I remember my first church family retreat. I had a room full of ten boys and I told them how much I had looked forward to this time with them. We stayed up very late and I explained to them it was now time to get some rest. I really stressed the need for their cooperation . . . it was already 2:00 a.m. and I expected them to go to sleep.

I came back from brushing my teeth and immediately had the strange sensation I was alone. Yep . . . my room was empty, the backdoor open to outside. I closed the door, turned out the light, and went to bed.

About an hour later the boys "snuck" back into the room barely disguising their glee. They wondered aloud how I could be so soft as to let them get away with it. There I was, sound asleep! The next morning I greeted them all pleasantly, and by breakfast time they were convinced they were in the clear. At breakfast I made the following speech to the whole retreat: "I really have enjoyed my cabin of boys, but I want them to know that all this is a privilege, not a right. Last night, my boys lost the privilege to have their own cabin, so tonight they'll get to sleep with their parents."

Dutifully, and with much remorse, the boys moved their stuff out after breakfast. The retreat and my relationship with the boys went great. I later heard they would privately coach newcomers to retreats with the words, "Len loves to have fun; he's great. But when he gives a rule, he means it. Don't cross him or you'll pay."

4. Surprise! If We Don't Like Them, They Won't Like Us. Young people give respect to a *person* in authority, not the position. If there ever was a day when young people had the attitude of "touch not the Lord's anointed," it has long since passed into oblivion. We have to earn the right to be heard. We have to earn the right to be respected.

Actually, this is one of the things I enjoy most about ministry with high schoolers. Each new crop of ninth graders cares nothing that I've been at the church thirteen years, have written some books, and speak to groups of youth pastors. All that means *zero* to them. What they want to know is if I love them, can they trust me, and am I real? If I don't, if we don't answer those questions right, we're in for trouble that could cut short our ministries.

> *"We fired Kent because he had the gift of guilt. Whenever he was up front, he was trying to make them feel guilty. He didn't talk to them personally, and showed little interest in them. He loved to lead things, and have kids obey his commands. It was like he was on some kind of power trip or something. If he could make a kid look foolish, it made him look better, or so he thought. Parents called us on the board to say that their kids didn't want to go to youth events any more. My kids gave up on him too, and they're normally really supportive."*

✱ ✱ ✱

Conflict, conflict everywhere. It's easy to get discouraged. As we look at ministry years ahead, it may seem like tiptoeing through a mine field. Yes, there will be conflicts. No, they don't have to ruin us or our ministries. Be patient, we'll get to the positive solutions soon. Remember, we are first trying to get a picture of the hazards ahead in ministry. We've looked at the first "Big C," now let's look at two more.

CHAPTER FOUR

COMPETENCY AND COMPROMISE

Thinking back, the sign behind the registration desk did strike me as being odd: "No illegal activities allowed on the premises." Having confirmed that the motel had received our full payment in the mail a month earlier, I walked back out to help the senior highers unload the church bus. The retreat was going great. We had slept on the floor of a church near Whistler Mountain, British Columbia, on Friday night, skied all day Saturday, and were excited about the rest of the weekend in the beautiful city of Vancouver, British Columbia. City Motel was now our headquarters.

A police car roared in from Main Street and stopped a yard from me. The officer got out and approached. Looking like he was confused, or lost, or something, he asked me: "What are you doing?"

"Well, officer," I replied, "As you see here, we're unloading the church bus. We're from Seattle, we were at Whistler today, and now we're going to stay here."

"Don't you know what this is?"

My life began to pass in front of me. "What do you mean?"

"This is a house of prostitution . . . serves this end of the city. Better keep a close watch on your kids."

"Thanks. . . ." My voice trailed off as he returned to his patrol car.

My mind was a blur . . . we had no money, there's no place else to stay, and most of the kids heard this conversation. No wonder City Motel was so cheap in the travel directory; just wait till news of this one gets out: "Youth pastor jailed for his own protection as angry parents picket church."

We moved into our rooms. They were so dirty most of the kids went right back to the bus to get their sleeping bags. The towels were paper-thin and stained. I gathered the group in my room and we talked about our predicament. We chose, with some discussion, to make the most of the situation. We had a good old-fashioned sing time and prayer meeting right there.

Just as the officer predicted, it was a very busy night. Male and female customers came and went all night long. Most of us didn't sleep very well. I was glad our bus driver was also an elder, so he could help me explain things back home. As far as I know, we're the only youth group in the history of the Christian and Missionary Alliance to have a retreat in a bordello.

All of us make mistakes. Sometimes it's funny at the time; sometimes it's funny only in retrospect. Most of us recover, learn our lesson, and go on. I never book a motel now unless I've seen it myself or have reliable reports about it.

Pity the poor youth worker who lost her job because she was goofing around with the girls at a retreat and took a picture of someone in the shower. Her senior pastor thought it was the most foolish prank he'd ever heard of and he fired her. Fortunately, most of us don't get the ax when we do something silly.

An occasional mistake is one thing. A pattern of bad choices, broken trust, and moral compromise will hurt or destroy our ministry. *Competency* and *compromise* are the second and third "Big C's" in which many youth workers get mired.

COMPETENCY: DO ANY OF THESE FIVE THINGS REGULARLY AND YOURS WILL BE QUESTIONED

Twenty percent of the fired youth pastors in my survey got fired because of incompetence. Being incompetent is likely to show up very early in a new ministry. As I pointed out earlier, 50 percent of the firings I surveyed had occurred in the first two years of a new ministry. If we show any of the following five things more than just occasionally, our ministry will be in deep trouble.

1. Laziness. Most churches who enjoy large staffs have expectations about office hours. Yes, if we are up till midnight the night before with kids, we're not expected to be at our desks at 8:00 a.m., but generally a regular schedule is the norm. If the office opens at

8:30 a.m., and we commonly saunter in two hours later, the word will spread.

"Good morning, this is Sunrise Community Church."

"Hello, this is Marge Smith. Is Pastor Terry in yet this morning?"

"No, I'm sorry he's not in. Can I take a message?"

"Do you know when he'll be in?"

"No, I'm sorry I don't; he didn't tell me."

"Never mind, I'll call back later."

"Why don't you try back around 10:30; he's usually in by then."

What is dear Mrs. Smith to think? Her husband scrapes himself out of bed at 5:30 a.m. and he's at his desk by 7:45. If Mrs. Smith has got another reason she's upset, our apparent laziness won't help improve our image. She, and others like her, may wonder what kind of scam we've got going.

Another cause for a laziness label to be attached to us is lack of initiative. There are certain basic tasks we must perform in ministry, but if that is all we do, we could be in trouble. On the other hand, if people see us trying new things and stretching with faith and vision for the benefit of the ministry, we won't be seen as lazy.

One of the nice things about being youth workers is that we are responsible for the use of our own time. We do not punch a time clock; we have no supervisor who knows exactly what we do on an hourly basis. Some youth pastors, though, cannot handle this freedom well. A work week of fifty to fifty-five hours is normal at the church I serve, but it would be very easy to get away with much less if I wanted to.

If we look lazy, we'll be thought of as incompetent.

2. Low Energy. Like it or not, youth ministry is by definition a high-energy occupation. We've got to have energy, and lots of it, if we hope to lead adolescents. Their bodies are pulsating with hormone-induced vitality. Being slow, unexpressive, or unenthusiastic will hurt our ministries. One parent lamented about her youth pastor, "I give Shari a good idea, and she said she'd do it, but then weeks pass and nothing happens. I feel like she's in slow motion most of the time. Ever tried to push a rope? That's what dealing with Shari is like."

Of course, we can get tired as youth workers. There may be personal crises that temporarily sap our energy from ministry. If slug speed is our norm, though, keeping the label of incompetence from sticking to us becomes increasingly difficult.

3. Punctuality.

> *"We fired Hal because he was always late. Honestly, he was late to Sunday school about 30 percent of the time. He was late to Wednesdays and socials sometimes, too. When he had a meeting with the volunteer staff or the youth leadership, he was usually late, too. The senior pastor spoke with him about this on several occasions. Basically, this habit destroyed his credibility with both kids and parents. We had no choice but to let him go."*

In Africa and South and Central America, missionaries adjust to cultures that have no sense of time urgency as we do in North America. Most of us, however, don't do youth ministry in Zimbabwe or Argentina; we do it here. Young people don't have much of a sense of time urgency either, but they do expect their leaders to be there when they say they'll be there.

One youth pastor dug a hole he never climbed out of by being undependable. He got the kids all excited about a youth choir . . . sixty-five kids showed up for the first rehearsal, and he was thirty minutes late. He was also late for the next two rehearsals. By the time he started being punctual, his choir was down to fifteen kids. The word from youth choir boycotters was, "Why should I commit to something when it's so obvious that Gene doesn't have his act together?"

4. Poor Judgment. One youth pastor was fired after he was arrested along with some of his high school boys. They were all throwing water balloons at cars late one night. *"Someone capable of making that big of a mistake has no place in ministry,"* was the comment on the survey.

Another youth pastor was fired after showing a video that was violent and sexual. We could argue that it was probably nothing

COMPETENCY AND COMPROMISE

worse than most kids *and* parents watch in the privacy of their own homes, yet it's certainly smarter to be cautious when it comes to movies.

I made a spectacular error in judgment on a backpacking trip one summer by allowing kids to jump off a fifty-five-foot cliff into a lake. Two of the five who did it were injured; one kid required immediate medical evacuation. Having been at the church over ten years, I didn't get fired . . . but it did cause conflict between me and the parents. A long and sincere letter of apology to all parents of senior high school kids was sufficient for most to forgive me.

Most churches will allow a rare judgment error, especially if it is followed by repentance and restoration. Make poor judgment a pattern, though, and storm clouds will gather overhead. Sooner or later lightning will strike and you'll be out of a job.

5. Lack of Organization. We could be awesome speakers. Our counseling ministry could be "two thumbs up." We could have a reputation for creative genius. We could be famous for our sincere godliness. All these are great, important, and needed. If we're not organized, though, we won't last long in ministry. Ever tried to build a deliciously messy banana split on a Kleenex? It can be done, but just try to pick that creation up and carry it somewhere! In the same way, our "creative genius" ministry will go nowhere if we can't learn at least some basic organizational skills.

If there were a Disorganized Youth Pastor Hall of Fame, the building (or complex of buildings) would have to be huge, and annually there would be hundreds of nominees. Here are a few excerpts from my survey that have signaled the end of another youth worker's ministry.

"Gary doesn't have an organized bone in his body."

"The last straw for Pastor Eric's ministry came when the youths hosted a church dinner and Eric forgot to have anyone prepare the main course. No kidding!"

"Leslie started out great as a youth pastor, but the group grew beyond her ability to manage; it all collapsed around her feet. She left a broken person."

"He didn't seem capable of sending the youth event schedule on time. There was no follow-through. He left details to the last minute. He forgot to arrange bus drivers for youth events. The kids thought he was a big joke."

"Janet left others in charge of an event, but forgot to inform them of that fact. Kids arrived, but no adults."

"Have you ever chaperoned a retreat and found the youth pastor did literally everything? He spoke, led singing, led games, did the cooking, washed the dishes, everything. Does he think we're so stupid that we can't even be trusted to help with meals?"

"He was a wonderful, godly person, loved by the pastor, board, and congregation. Firing him was very painful. He simply did not belong in ministry. Organizational skills were totally nonexistent."

"Incompetent in what areas? All."

I too have had my struggles in this area. In my first church after seminary, I did pretty well in organizing and managing the people-resources God had entrusted to me. It was management by luck, grace, and a smile, however. I carried this approach to my second church, a ministry double the size of the first, and soon people on the youth staff began resigning. The disturbing thing was . . . they all gave similar reasons. "You don't keep me informed enough." "I don't feel needed." "This is a one-man show after all." "Do you know what you're doing?" Not exactly comforting words for someone committed to long-term youth ministry.

The big crisis for me came when a board member took me to lunch and gave me the news.

"Len, I've been on your youth staff a year. I think you really know what you're doing when it comes to kids. But you have no idea what to do when it comes to adults. This weakness is killing your ministry effectiveness and you've got to change."

It was the most nutritional lunch I've ever had when it comes to ministry growth. The church sent me to some management seminars, I read lots of books, and went back to the internal drawing board.

We've described ministry incompetence. It's something that can keep us from getting through the first couple of years, let alone the next five or ten. In Chapters Eight and Nine, we'll get past description and move on to prescription . . . medicine for the unorganized youth worker.

Now we will turn to the dark side of youth ministry.

MORAL COMPROMISE

As we begin our first years in ministry we feel certain we could never become a casualty because of compromise. That may happen to others, but not to us . . . we're called by God, fired up to serve him, and convinced of our own pure heart. It's the personal myth revisited. We see this attitude in young people ("Others may get killed when they drink and drive, not me."), but us . . . no . . . it could never happen to *us*. Very few rookie youth workers understand how hard it is to remain upright in a moral terrain as slippery as ministry. Of those who lose their jobs in youth ministry, nearly 18 percent do so because of moral compromise.

1. How Much Money Is Enough? Just a Little Bit More. Most youth workers handle lots of money. Kids turn in retreat money to us. We collect gas money on the bus during a day trip. T-shirt sales, fund raisers, special offerings . . . much of it comes to us. It may pause on our desk for a day, week, or month until we turn it in, but it's up to us and our integrity to make sure it gets deposited in the proper account.

Youth ministry firings due to money are rare. One youth worker lost his job because he was supporting an addiction with funds from the youth group checking account, over which he had sole control. Although actual job terminations over mishandling money may be rare, many youth workers struggle with money.

Youthworker journal did a random sample of 500 of their subscribers on a wide range of ethical issues. Here are the findings:[1]

Money, especially too little of it, is a big
problem for me.   39 percent

I have used church money or youth group
money for personal expenses.   19 percent

I have turned in expense forms for reimburse-
ment from my church for personal stuff.   7 percent

I have stretched some income tax loopholes far
enough to call it cheating.   5 percent

Some made additional comments about money.

"Low salaries create tremendous ethical pressure."

"I rationalize the spending of church time/money for personal use because they owe it to me."

Even if we have high personal integrity when it comes to handling youth group money, it is easy to become careless. Church treasurers and financial secretaries like receipts, financial summary statements, and other financial paper trails that we must be able to provide. More on this in Chapter Ten.

2. How Much Sex Is Enough? Just a Little Bit More. In my survey, 15 percent of youth pastors were fired because of sexual impropriety. Both *Leadership* and *Youthworker* have surveyed their subscribers about sex. Given the moral tone of this day, the numbers aren't very shocking, but they are sobering. Most of those who responded to the *Leadership* survey were senior pastors. We will look at those numbers first, then youth workers. From *Leadership*:[2]

Since I have been in local church ministry
I have done something with someone (not my   23 percent
spouse) that I feel was sexually inappropriate.

I have had sexual intercourse with someone
other than my spouse since I've been in   12 percent
ministry.

I have had other forms of sexual contact
with someone other than my spouse
(passionate kissing, mutual   18 percent
masturbation/fondling) since I've been
in local church ministry.

If you have had intercourse outside of
marriage, with whom did you do it?
     counselee   17 percent
     ministerial staff member   5 percent
     other church staff member   8 percent
     church lay leader   9 percent
     someone else in congregation   30 percent
     someone outside congregation   31 percent

What have been the personal consequences
of your sexual contact?
     divorce   6 percent
     other marriage problems   16 percent
     loss of job   6 percent

My church has become aware of my sexual
contact.   4 percent

I fantasize sexually
     daily   6 percent
     weekly   20 percent
     monthly   35 percent

Leadership also surveyed 1,000 evangelical Christian lay people and found that their statistics were roughly double that of the pastors in each category.

The *Youthworker* survey did not ask the same questions as the *Leadership* survey, but the results do provide us with a picture of how widespread sexual impropriety is:[3]

Sexual temptation is a big problem for me.	32 percent
I sometimes look at pornographic magazines or films.	26 percent
After becoming a Christian, I have had an inappropriate sexual encounter with someone.	31 percent
I have had a sexual encounter with a member of my youth group.	2 percent

I do not want to be guilty of fostering cerebral voyeurism, but it is important, I think, to be shocked and saddened by what we are actually capable of doing. This will help motivate us to build fences around ourselves, to protect ourselves from a moral mistake that costs us our conscience and our ministry.

My research files contain many horror stories. Here are a few (the real names are not used, of course).

Mitch started having sexual relations with the senior pastor's high school daughter. His wife left him, the church fired him, and he left town swearing he'd return for this sixteen-year-old girl . . . his one true love. Another church hired him (!!) and, unrepentant, he still vows to return for the pastor's daughter.

Alex lost his job when it was revealed that he wrote sexually explicit love notes to a fifteen-year-old.

Edward convinced his church he had nearly finished medical school before becoming a pastor. His purported specialty was gynecology. Over a period of several years he became close to many girls in the senior high group and "ministered" to them by physically examining them. Some of these sessions led to sexual relations. When one of the girls came forward with the truth, the church was stunned to learn how many were actually involved. Edward was a master at deception, cover up, and covert behavior.

Neil's church, for some reason, did not fire him when the youth group girl with whom he'd been having sexual intercourse told the story to her parents. They did fire him a few months later after he was arrested for pretending to be a police officer. He picked up prostitutes and forced them to have sex. One of the prostitutes turned him in!

Reading these stories makes my soul shudder. *Most* of the people described above began their ministries with a pure heart and a sincere love for God and his kingdom. They led Bible studies, prayed with and for kids, and exhorted their young people to holy living. The tragic facts, however, speak for themselves. Some started out as spectacularly as a space shuttle liftoff, but a short time later they had self-destructed, spreading human wreckage through families, the church, and beyond. As we survey this damage, our hearts long to turn toward prevention and cure. How can we keep ourselves from the same catastrophes?

* * *

We have looked at the three "Big C's" : compromise, competence, and conflict. We have also considered other poisons toxic to ministry health, especially during the first five years: SAD; the morale curve; idealism; and personal change. We have described the problems. Now let's look at positive ideas that will help us build fences against failure and equip us to make it.

PART TWO

ESSENTIAL SKILLS: BUILDING FENCES AGAINST FAILURE

CHAPTER FIVE

WORKING POSITIVELY WITH YOUR PASTOR

Robert Hochheiser's book, *How To Work For a Jerk,* begins:

> If you think the person you work for is described in this book, you're wrong. Any resemblance between the persons portrayed on the following pages and real life bosses is strictly coincidental. . . . *My objective here is to help you understand what bosses are, and to show you how to circumvent what they do.* . . . This book has been written with your needs in mind if you are laboring under the impression that your boss has succeeded despite being a jerk. Millions of people feel like that. . . .
>
> I'm about to show you not only why bosses act like jerks, but how they get away with it, *how you can do the same, and how you can prevent them from succeeding at your expense.*[1]

The book is affectionately dedicated "To the Bosses of the World: Without whom I wouldn't have been exposed to the pettiness and stupidity that inspired this book."

Youth pastors are not the only ones who can have trouble with their bosses. It's an all too common problem in the world of work. If we're searching for the smoking gun of reasons why youth pastors get fired or resign, this is it. Conflict with the senior pastor shoots down many a ministry and, of those who got fired, it was the most frequent cause (42 percent) listed on my survey.

It's not surprising that this should be the case. Our pastors want a "successful" church. A successful church has to have a dynamic youth ministry . . . everyone expects it. When things go wrong in our department, the senior pastor eventually hears about it, and he or she may even hear about it *before we do.* The office of the senior pastor is a clearinghouse, an ecclesiastical funnel, through which passes bad news about us. There can come a point when the quantity of bad news finally tips the balance against us, and we've got ourselves into major conflict with our boss.

It doesn't have to be this way. Many youth pastors enjoy great relationships with their senior pastors. I've had four senior pastors: one at my first church and three at my second. Each one has been an excellent friend. Initiative on our part will help make the senior pastor our ally instead of our enemy. We must, by God's grace, (1) understand them, (2) have integrity ourselves, and (3) build bridges.

UNDERSTANDING OUR SENIOR PASTORS

Philosophy of Ministry and Vision. The tension level went from low to high in just thirty seconds. We were evaluating the previous Sunday morning service. All of us (we thought) felt it had gone very well and we were about to move on to the next agenda item. Then our junior high pastor chimed in.

"But we didn't present the Gospel."

"Well Frank, we did try to interest people in becoming Christians, and those who are hungry will come back," our senior pastor replied.

"But there was no plan of salvation."

"There doesn't need to be; we didn't have 'visitor Sunday' to give the impression that we exist to jam the Bible down their throats," added our visitation pastor.

"There should have been a Gospel presentation and an altar call. The reason this church isn't growing is because we never present the Gospel and ask people to respond," Frank persisted.

A short agenda item turned into a long one, as a clear philosophy of ministry difference had been exposed.

How close are you in agreement with your senior pastor when it comes to issues of ministry philosophy? React to the following statements for yourself and for your pastor.[2] If you strongly agree, write in "10." If you strongly disagree, write in "1." A "6" means you slightly agree, while a "4" means you slightly disagree.

(a) The church will grow best if it *targets* the population it is trying to reach (baby boomers, for example), instead of consciously trying to reach everyone.
My score:_____   My pastor's score:_____

(b) The pastors should dynamically lead the church, as opposed to hanging back and equipping the people to lead for themselves.
My score:_____   My pastor's score:_____

(c) The Sunday morning sermon should be aimed at non-Christians primarily, and that Christian nurture takes place in a different setting.
My score:_____   My pastor's score:_____

(d) Evangelism should be organized and structured by the church for its people, not just left to happen haphazardly.
My score:_____   My pastor's score:_____

(e) Bible teaching should emphasize practical principles for life. This is much more productive than nebulous teaching about "the Lord working through us."
My score:_____   My pastor's score:_____

(f) The worship service should be like a heavenly party, rather than meditative and reflective.
My score:_____   My pastor's score:_____

(g) The youth pastor and the senior pastor should have a close, supportive friendship.
My score:_____   My pastor's score:_____

All this material is dynamite information—if we are smart enough to figure it out in the candidating process. It is easy to see that if our pastor teaches "The Bible as Principle" and we're starving for the "Christ life," we are in for stomach upset Sunday after Sunday. If we deeply feel the pastor should be the dynamic leader/keeper of the vision, and he sees himself as a laid-back facilitator, we're bound to be in conflict.

Although it helps youth workers *most* to try to figure this out in advance, it still helps us gain understanding of our boss if we figure it out while we are actually in ministry, too.

It's okay not to agree with our senior pastor on all parts of the above quiz. In fact, total agreement is probably rare. In cases of disagreement, however, it is up to us to determine if we can live with the difference of opinion. We might not much care that our boss wants to reach yuppies, and we'd like to see the congregation mixed up a little bit. But we might die if we're looking for preaching with "solid principles to live by" and all we get is "live in his strength." If our philosophy of ministry difference is deep enough, to have integrity, it may mean that we have to start looking for a different place of ministry (more on this in Chapter Thirteen).

As important as philosophy of ministry, is vision. It's important to believe in the vision of the pastor or, if it doesn't come from that source, then the vision of the church leadership. Another source of conflict is if we are looking for vision and there is none to be found.

As to philosophy of ministry and vision, Confucius didn't say it, but I sure believe it: "The One Who Figures This Out Will Smile More Than The One Who Doesn't."

The Seasons of a Man's Life. Adult development is not continuous. It is incremental and occurs in stages. Understanding where your senior pastor is in the process of "growing up" may help explain some of the ways he approaches life and ministry. It also helps us to understand our own progress in the journey of growing up, as well. According to David Levinson in *The Seasons of a Man's Life*,[3] here is how it happens, at least for males.

Age (in years)

17-22	Early adult transition. Move out of preadult world.
23-28	Entering adult world. Explore this adult world and create a stable life structure.
29-33	Transition. "Life is real; it's serious."
34-40	Settling down. Focus on "making it."

41-45   Mid-life transition/crises. "Now that it's half over, what have I done with my life? What's next?"
46-50   Settling down again.
51-55   Transition again. "Old age isn't so far off, any more!"
56-60   Settle down.
61-65   Last transition. Coming to grips with age.

Understanding these stages can help us a great deal. Want to know why your sixty-two-year-old pastor won't support adding a second morning worship service? Too risky. Men in that age group don't usually risk much. Curious about why your fifty-year-old boss has turned quiet? After fifty comes *sixty* and that's *old*. It's a sobering thought!

Looking for a reason to pray for your forty-two-year-old chief? Pray that he'll resist the temptation of adultery. Many men and many pastors his age, fearing loss of sexual prowess, throw away both ministry and marriage, happily exchanging an ounce of pleasure for a pound of pain as they run off with a woman twenty years younger. Wonder why your thirty-seven-year-old pastor is such a hard driver? He's *making his mark,* and those denominational big shots better notice!

If you have a female senior pastor, don't miss reading Jean Lush's *The Emotional Phases of a Woman's Life.*[4] Lush expertly describes the implications of the menstrual month with its "seasons." If your female senior pastor hasn't gone through menopause yet, she's still susceptible to the menstral cycle. The days before her period are like deep winter and she is likely to be touchy, depressed, or critical. Spring follows quickly, however, and in that week there's no limit to her emotional energy. Summer follows with continued energy, and positive feelings. The climate changes, however, as summer slides into fall, with an ensuing lack of energy and a negative undertow. Now this is a lot of emotional weather to pack into twenty-eight days, but according to Lush, these are the facts.

Furthermore, if your female senior pastor is between the ages of thirty-seven and forty-five, she could also be weighted down by the "mid-life malaise." Here, a woman begins to feel like she's coming unglued mentally. Some women have virtually no negative symptoms during these years, although others experience a dark cloud over their personalities that seldom leaves.

Of course, not all men and not all women will fit neatly into these scholarly categories, but all the academic and literary energy expended on adult transitions is not fantasy. Christians, and Christian leaders, grow up, too! These age-related pressures create an emotional undertow that may go largely unseen by us. Broad tendencies, however, may be noticed and attributed to the seasons.

Other Pressures. We must remember that our pastor is a man or woman under pressure. When people have complaints about the church, they usually take them to the top . . . no, not God . . . they take them to the senior pastor. And people can be less than kind.

Additionally, there are the issues of noses and nickels. If your pastor is normal, he makes sure both are counted accurately. He feels good if the noses and nickels are up from the year before. He is uneasy if they're not. He is deeply insecure if they're down. One reason the senior pastor has employed us is to make these two statistics climb. "Senior pastors may glibly say at staff meetings that 'numbers are not important,' but that doesn't alter the fact that large and hyperactive youth groups are prerequisites to their own images as successes."[5]

Working positively with our senior pastors means we must first try to understand them. We must understand us, too!

INTEGRITY AS A STAFF MEMBER

> *"I asked the board to fire Brian because he was undermining my ministry as senior pastor. After being here just three months, he had a list of things about the whole church he wanted to change. He freely gave his opinion about my weaknesses to others in the congregation. He said I didn't have the right personality to lead a church successfully. I couldn't trust him anymore. He told some members of the youth group he wanted to be senior pastor someday."*

The confessions of an insecure senior pastor? Maybe. If these charges are true, however, this youth pastor was behaving very immaturely. Integrity was lacking. What does it mean to have integrity as a youth pastor?

We Understand We're Not Number One. We must face the fact squarely and honestly—as youth pastors we are not in charge of the church. We are under authority. We do not have the last word, we do not have the final say, and our great wisdom may not even be consulted on some church-wide issues.

Just like some of our don't-pet-my-fur-the-wrong-way young people feel, we tense up when forced to accept the leadership of the head pastor. Were we strong willed as young people? Were we second born in our families? Our past gives us clues about problems we may have with authority.

Tony Campolo observes that youth pastors try to do an end run around their pastors by (1) displaying their more up-to-date education, (2) casting the senior pastor as "keeper of the status quo," and (3) using youth ministry to climb the denominational big-shot ladder.[6]

To have integrity as youth pastors, we must abandon our craving for power and the games we use to get it. Yes, our education may be more recent than our boss'. Yes, the senior pastor may be a jerk when it comes to lack of vision. And we may, if we're exceptionally good as youth pastors, find denominational or national recognition. Our *heart* is what matters here.

Jesus clearly rejected the world's view of status and prestige. If we want to have his view, then we must have the attitude of a servant (Matt. 20:25-28). By God's grace and his strength in us we must learn to be content where we are and in the positions we are in (Phil. 4:10-13).

I've struggled with this. Although all the senior pastors I've worked for have been good ones, and I've been a friend to each, two were especially weak where I was strong. I'm a planner and an organizer. I plan things in my sleep and wake up in the morning with some daunting project laid out in exquisite detail. With one pastor, I constantly felt frustrated because he made long-range planning mistakes. It was even more frustrating because I was always right. It was very hard not to "lord it over" both him and others in this regard. God had to deal severely with my proud and hard heart.

My attitude and heart had made some progress by the time another "Main Man" came on the scene. About the future and planning I said little, and I just concentrated on the youth ministry. This pastor then blew me away by saying, "It's obvious to me you've got a gift when it comes to vision and planning. I'd like you to tell me what we should do, and I'll take it to the board. You do the dreaming, I'll carry it out." Was I excited? Well . . . is water wet? Do birds fly? Do flowers bloom in spring? My spirit soared for only a few weeks, however, before bad news shot that dream out of the sky. My pastor was diagnosed with cancer; he died nine months later.

Communication Quicksand. A second part of our integrity as a staff member deals with how we handle negative feelings about our boss, both in ourselves and in what we hear from others.

If we hear someone complaining about the senior pastor, we must exhort them that it is not right to complain to others without first talking with him or her. Or, if it is misinformation the person is reacting to, we can set them straight.

About our own negative feelings, sensitivity is required. Pondering the pressures our pastor is under, and thinking about where he or she is when it comes to life's seasons, has usually caused me to keep silent and just pray.

In one case, I did bring to the pastor an observation . . . that the young people were ridiculing him because of a particularly odd and distracting gesture he made when he preached. He told me later that he was inwardly very angry with me for telling him, but that eventually he was grateful. By the way, he discontinued using that gesture.

Say Only Good in Public. A cousin of the last point, this aspect of youth pastor integrity is vital. There is good in every senior pastor. There is something to praise, something to admire.

It's nice when our boss has the same ideas we do. One pastor said to his new youth minister, "I want you to know that when we are in public, I will be behind you 100 percent . . . without exception. No matter what other people say to me about you, regardless of what you might have done, they will learn quickly that you are my man for youth ministry in this church and that I am supporting you. Now, that doesn't mean that we won't have our differences, and privately we might really need to hash them out in a big way. But it does mean that you can count on me to be your number one advocate in this church and in this community."[7]

May his tribe increase!

BUILDING BRIDGES

One of my favorite meetings of the month is the "Third Wednesday." About twelve of us youth pastors gather to laugh, share, discuss, worship, and pray. Recently we spent an hour talking about getting along with our bosses. I took some notes. Here is a slice of that conversation.

Kevin: For me it starts with prayer. I've got to pray for my boss . . . all the pressures he faces.

Bonnie: Yeah, that's fine, but you gotta spend time together as a staff. Otherwise you won't even know what to pray about.

Len: Our staff got a lot closer when we decided to take an hour each week outside of staff meetings just to pray for each other. That meant we had to be honest and get below the surface.

Bonnie: I'll say again the basis of good prayer, though, is relationship. Our staff goes on an outing about once a quarter. We might go for a day hike in the summer, out to a nice restaurant in the winter, that sort of thing. It's lots of fun.

Len: We tried a staff hike once, and our counseling pastor complained all the way there and all the way back. We've never let him live it down. His idea of an outing is to go outside and sit in a hot tub.

Kevin: I try to look for ways to encourage my pastor.

Bonnie: I'm open for ideas on that one.

Kevin: When I think he preaches a good sermon, I tell him so. I appreciate the way he goes to bat for me at the board level, too. Sometimes my wife makes him an apple pie, and we leave it on his desk with a thank-you note.

Mike: Sounds corny.

Kevin: Corny or not, it works.

George: Isn't there a verse about that in Hezekiah? Just kidding! I helped the kids toilet paper his office on his birthday. I knew he'd take it well and see it as a sign of love.

Bonnie: T.p.'d his office, ha! That's child's play. We've t.p.'d his house! We helped him clean it up, though.

Mike: Our youth group holds an annual "Pastor Roast." We do some funny skits about our pastor and what we think he must have been like as a teenager. The time ends with some sincere words of thanks, plus prayer for him and his family.

Bonnie: Do any of you have nicknames for your boss?

Kevin: I don't think my boss would appreciate it.

George: I've named my pastor "Augustus." I think a good nickname is a sign of affection. One of the things that has built bridges the most with my senior pastor is that he knows I support and accept him. He knows he's not perfect. I know he's not perfect. He knows that I know. I know that he knows that I . . . just kidding! Anyway, we accept each other for what we are and consciously try to help each other. I really try to communicate with him also. He's on my youth and parent mailing list. If something goes wrong, I make sure he hears about it from me first.

Len: We named one senior pastor on our staff "Big Toad." It stuck. The congregation loved it. Then we had "Personal Toad," "Adolescent Toad," "Children's Toad," and "Musical Toad." We didn't put it on the letterhead, though.

Dave: I've been silent through all this—I guess it's because I'm jealous. My boss is distant, aloof. He's nearly ready to retire and I guess he was raised in an era that wasn't so open and free. I'm not sure he knows what fun is.

Bonnie: So this has been a big adjustment for you. It hasn't been what you'd expected.

Dave: Right. It's not that I've written him off. I do compliment him, and pray for him. If I t.p.'d his office, he'd be dumbfounded and confused. I just realize that this is the way it's going to be; he's not going to change. I have a lot of joy in the youth ministry and get lots of encouragement from the youth staff and the parents. I don't look to my boss for support, 'cause if I did, I'd just be disappointed. I don't blame him for the way he is.

Bonnie: Sounds like you're on top of this one.

Dave: I think so. When I was a candidate, it was pretty obvious what his style was. I felt God leading me to the church and I'm thankful for all the good in my pastor and my church—and I try to overlook what isn't so perfect.

* * *

Time, encouragement, not laying blame, being content, lots of prayer, good communication, empathetic understanding . . . these are all important components of a good relationship with the senior pastor. When we get this mastered we take a huge step in ministry happiness.

However . . . there's more. We've got to work well with the parents, too. One of the hard things about parents is that occasionally they're right! Let's consider them now and how to work positively with them.

CHAPTER SIX

WORKING POSITIVELY
WITH PARENTS

"Pastor Len, I can't believe you did this," began Mrs. Carlson.

My adrenaline started to rise. Another in a series of tense exchanges. "You told us parents that Roger was one of the chaperones. I let Sara go on the trip based on the fact that there was at least one adult there whom I could trust . . . not just college kids."

Mentally, I was heading for my bunker. The college visitation weekend had a year's worth of problems packed into one miserable weekend. Roger had phoned only two days before the trip to let me know he really couldn't go. Though I was not going on the trip, I felt confident that we did have sufficient staff along, including the youth pastor of another church. The kid/staff ratio met our guidelines. Mrs. Carlson continued.

"When I got to the church and saw that everything had been changed, I felt like you had lied. You say one thing, and then do another. I was so angry . . . you took away any control or option I had as a parent. I almost didn't let Sara get on the bus, but that would have created a big scene in the parking lot."

One of my policies is: "When in doubt, apologize."

"I understand how you would feel, Mrs. Carlson, by being surprised when you saw the staffing change. There was nothing I could do about Roger backing out. We had enough adults going to meet our guidelines. I really apologize for . . ."

"Your apologies mean nothing, Len. Apologies are cheap; then you go on your own merry way. I don't count college kids as staff, and you know that. They don't have near the maturity, and you know that. And when I heard that the bus broke down four times, and that they drove with a possibility of brake failure. . . ."

After this conversation, I stared out the window for a long while. Damage-control time. "If you can't stand the heat, get out of the kitchen," I reminded myself. "I wonder if Grace Church still needs a youth pastor. Hmmm, I wish I was filthy rich and didn't have to work at all. Retiring thirty years early might be fun." And so I mused. Eventually I was able to pray about my feelings and get back on my feet.

I wondered if Mrs. Carlson's tsunami of anger was going to be the worst, or if there were higher waves yet to follow. I've learned that parental reactions to youth ministry misfortune vary from case to case. Sometimes the worst reactions come first. Sometimes the first is only a faint hint of the wrath that is to come. This time none of the other parents were *that* upset. The Carlsons left the church a few months later, as did the Transportation Committee Chairman, upon whom parental anger about the church bus was vented.

And so it goes when working with parents . . . we win some and we lose some. Some will rise up and call us blessed. Others will rise up and call for our execution. As we work positively with our senior pastor, so it should be with parents. We need to (1) understand them, (2) have integrity ourselves, and (3) build bridges.

UNDERSTANDING PARENTS

Parenting isn't child's play. It can be hard, frustrating, and unrewarding. To get through the early years in our first church, or any church, we must pay attention to parents' feelings, needs, and desires. To make our youth ministry work, this is crucial. To ignore parents is to invite conflict with them and guarantee our ministry with young people will not be complete. We *can* work successfully with parents. Yes, it's easier at age forty than at age nineteen, but it is still possible to have a credible ministry with parents, even if we are barely out of high school ourselves.

Know and understand this: over 80 percent of the parents in your church feel that their job as a parent is difficult, and much more difficult than when their parents were raising a family.[1] Why?

Times Have Changed. James Dobson asked his dad, "Do you remember worrying about me as a kid? Did you think about all the things that could go wrong as I came through the teenage years?"

His dad's reply? "Honestly, I never gave it much thought."[2]

Our grandparents and, if we're older than twenty-five, probably our parents, were raised in a rural or small town setting. Or, even if they were raised in a city, the neighborhood had a small town feel. Relatives were everywhere. "Gosh, if Uncle Gus knew I did that, he'd kill me!" In this environment, bad news about a kid's misbehavior traveled back to parents faster than a FAX. The extended family and community expectations held children in a sticky web of behavioral expectations. It was easier to raise kids: everyone knew what was expected, the kids couldn't get away with much misbehavior, and parents received lots of help raising them from relatives, neighbors, and the community at large. Yes, some young people rebelled, but most did not.

Today's parents are functioning solo. The grandparents live a thousand miles away, families change addresses about as often as they change cars, and that "sticky web of expectations" hardly exists. Opportunities for teenage misbehavior have mushroomed. Consider this—just about any teenager in America can watch virtually explicit sex using a VCR. When their parents were teenagers, the VCR hadn't been invented. Yes, times have changed! Raising kids seems harder now.

Lifecycles and Seasons. None of the parents in our churches have *any* previous experience being the ages they are. At ages thirty-five to fifty-five, they are experiencing many personal pressures. Eighty percent of them feel they are in the wrong job.[3] One major study of 15,000 executives showed that 75 percent were contemplating, going through, or recovering from divorce.[4] Some fathers will be feeling the undertow of a mid-life crisis. Mothers are not exempt from the dark side, either. Some of them will experience the "mid-life malaise" I discussed in Chapter Five.[5] Their own parents will experience failing health and death. Many of the youth group parents in our churches will feel this burden and loss deeply, and it can have profound effects on their ability to parent and function well.

That's not all. Parents in our churches are beginning to deal with their own poor health . . . cancer, heart disease, chronic ailments.

As the inescapable evidence mounts, parents conclude that their bodies will not last forever . . . they are mortal.

Marital Stresses of Parenthood. Add to this gloomy picture a strong willed teenager or two, and the life-satisfaction feeling in the home plummets. I long ago lost count of how many parents I have seen grieve over the rebelliousness of their teenagers. Many of those parents also struggle with their marriages as a result. What to do about Debbie on drugs or Pam who's pregnant or Dan who's frequently drunk? Unanimity can come hard for these couples.

Tired and Guilty. Single parents struggle to do it all alone. Husbands and wives struggle to make ends meet. Many of the mothers in our churches are "second shift moms" . . . they work all day and then try to do a day's worth of housework or shopping when they get home.[6] As these pressures mount, both parents are spending less time with their kids—considerably less than *their* parents did.[7] They know their kids need them, but they feel powerless about how to make it happen.

Open to Help. The *upside* of all this downside is parents know they need help. Large churches that can afford quality youth programs usually see an influx of Christian families. A small church with no youth group is fine when the children are little. When Johnny and Judy start hitting the upper elementary years, however, parents start to panic. They want a church that will offer solid ministry for their kids . . . and for them, too, if possible. What, specifically, do Christian parents want?

Search Institute's founder Dr. Merton Strommen's research tells us that Christian parents want five things.[8]

1. To understand themselves and their kids.
2. To have a close family.
3. To see their kids behave morally.
4. To have a sense of shared faith with their kids.
5. To have access to outside help.

Number five is where we come in. Our churches have parents who are hurting, hopeful, and expecting that the youth group will be a meaningful part of their kids' lives. They come to us wanting help themselves, too. We must, repeat, we *must* consider parents in our youth ministry.

Before we can do this, however, we have to have personal integrity with respect to parents.

YOUTH WORKER'S PERSONAL INTEGRITY

Coming to Terms with the Parents' Point of View. Especially if we are under twenty-five, understanding and appreciating the parents' point of view can be very difficult. A sign of personal integrity and maturity in ministry is when we consciously consider the parental perspective in our decisions.

> *"We fired our youth pastor because he only acted like a big kid. There was no separation between the kids and how they acted and him. This guy acted like a sixteen-year-old and soon both the kids and the parents wanted him out."*

There are many positive, practical things we can do that will demonstrate to parents that we understand their point of view.

A concern for *safety* is a big one.

I was nineteen when I was hired by a church to be their junior high youth director. That I was totally oblivious to parental concerns became quickly apparent, as the following example illustrates.

I was deeply in love with my new Camaro. One Friday evening I packed eleven junior high school kids (no kidding) in that car and went cruising. Have you ever seen how small a Camaro really is on the inside? There were five of us in the front and seven in the back. Funny thing, the patrolman who pulled me over didn't think it was very funny. Neither did the parents who heard about it.

It may not come naturally, but we *must* think about safety to have integrity as a youth pastor. Youth workers who want to drive the church vehicles like F16 fighter pilots need not apply.

The parents' point of view involves *the clock* as well. We can have integrity when we end our youth meetings and events when we say they will end. Sure, an occasional mistake here is not a problem. Make it a pattern, though, and our stock goes down.

Asking parents *how they think and feel* about the youth program can show that we care about their point of view. One youth pastor tried to make personal contact with each parent each year, just to ask for their opinions and feedback. She was young, but the parents learned to respect her.

Whose Side Are We On? As youth pastors we hear a lot of negative things about parents from kids. That is not surprising. But if *we* always speak about them as the bad guys, we lack integrity. We may not want to admit it, but most parents are right most of the time when it comes to their kids. They know them better than we do, they love them more than we do, and their relationship with them will continue long after we have left the scene. Yes, parents do and say unbelievably stupid things to their teenagers, but they are not always wrong.

We can gain parental respect if we tell them we want to partner with them in ministry to their teenager.

Some youth workers have trouble getting along with parents because they have trouble getting along with adults in general. Much of this interaction will be determined by how well we got along with our own parents.

How We Get Along with Our Own Parents. Paul Thigpen tells the story of a youth worker named Josh. "His complaints were always the same: The pastor and the church were rigid and old fashioned; they never allowed him the freedom to make his own decisions. Though the kids loved him, their parents did not respect him. Everyone was critical of him, he said . . . even his wife.

"During one of his complaining sessions, I decided to ask Josh a few questions about his parents. Josh's turbulent adolescence had been a rebellion against a tyrannical father and a critical mother. After college he had moved across the country to escape them, but somehow they seemed to have come along in his emotional baggage. His wife had begun to remind of him of his mother, and the senior pastor was 'just like' his father. . . . He found himself resenting any kind of authority, reacting fiercely to criticism, and feeling more like one of the kids than one of the adults."[9]

Is negative parental baggage hurting our ministry? Thigpen's questionnaire can help us. Put a check mark by each statement that is generally true for you.

In My Youth Ministry

___I automatically side with kids in my group who are in conflict with parents.

___I frequently feel resentment toward the parents of my kids.

___I criticize parents when talking with kids.

___I have frequent conflicts with those in authority over me . . . senior pastor, church council, or board of deacons.

___I tend to look to senior staff members as parent figures and feel frustrated when they don't meet my emotional needs.

___I look to my kids to give me a sense of acceptance and approval, but find that even when they give it, I'm not satisfied.

___I frequently feel left out, unappreciated, or taken for granted by other staff members.

In My Personal Life

___I see the same problems emerging in my marriage that I had with my parent of the opposite sex.

___I have a persistent struggle with anger.

___I find myself treating my own children in ways I disliked being treated as a child.

___I dread having to call, write, or visit my parents.

___I regress to a childhood or adolescent role when I visit my parents.

___I still compare myself to a sibling.

___I frequently feel disappointed or bitter about work, family, relationships, God, or life in general.

If many of these are generally true for us, we've got parental baggage that is definitely hurting us. If this is who we are, we need to begin to work toward resolution and healing. Paul Thigpen suggests the following steps as a place to begin:

1. Make a list of your parents' offenses against you.
2. Remember your offenses against them.
3. Find someone to listen to all this.
4. Understand your parents.
5. Forgive your parents and yourself.
6. Begin to assume responsibility for your life.

We try to understand parents; we decide to make personal integrity with parents a high priority. Both these acts give us a good foundation to build on with the parents of our youth group kids.

BUILDING BRIDGES

Our role with parents, even if we ourselves are barely out of adolescence, can be that of resource person, trainer, discipler, friend, and encourager.[10] There are many practical things we can do.

Newsletters, monthly or at least quarterly, will give parents the message that we want to be in touch. Newsletters can talk about upcoming events, ask for prayer, and present helpful material to parents. I love to use Jay Kesler's *Parents and Teenagers* as a real gold mine when it comes to short, helpful, and practical input for parents.[11] We shouldn't kid ourselves, however. Many parents won't take the time to read what we send them. At least, though, we can't be accused of not trying.

Parent Meetings and *Parent/Teen Socials* can be effective tools that build bridges, even if they happen only once a year.

Parent Seminars will be very appreciated by some. No, we don't have to lead them. Good resources are available now on video, or we can call in an expert. *Parent Panels* can be real winners . . . subjects like "Rules, In-Hours, Behavior Expectations" will be enjoyed. Parents love to compare notes on these things.

Parent Support Groups will be hungered for by those whose young people are in complete rebellion. *Parent Prayer Groups* can meet a similar need.

Want to be considered brilliant by parents and have them sing your praises to their friends? Look at the above smorgasbord of ideas, get out your calendar, and lay out your plan for the whole year. Get it laser printed at the copy shop on quality paper, and mail it to the parents. Do this in your first two months of ministry at a new church and some will want to build a shrine in your honor. As you carry out this plan during the year, recruit a team of parents who will plan *and carry out with you* the next year's plan. Make pleasing parents a high priority and you'll take a huge step in making your ministry work.

I have learned some of these things the hard way through the years. In my eleventh summer as youth pastor here, we had several things go wrong in the senior high ministry. We had some accidents, close calls, and a series of other problems that alarmed some parents. It alarmed me, too. On the advice of my wife, I called together a committee of ten parents. We came up with a staffing and safety document, sent it to all the parents for comment, revised it, had it approved by the Christian Education Committee, and sent the final version out to all the parents. It was reviewed and approved by our senior high youth leadership as well.

Though not exactly scintillating reading, this policy statement built two kinds of bridges for me. It helped parents have confidence in how the youth ministry was being conducted. Second, it built a bridge with my staff members . . . people who help with the youth groups range in age from nineteen to fifty. All of us know and understand these guidelines. I share the whole document with you because there might be something that will be helpful in your specific ministry situation.

Youth Ministry Safety and Staffing Guidelines for Activities[12]

The leaders of the youth ministry are free to schedule outdoor activities that are "normal" for young people and their parents. This includes snow skiing, swimming, hiking, camping, going on retreats, to amusement parks, and similar activities. This *excludes* hang gliding, skydiving, mountain climbing, rock climbing, cliff jumping, white water rafting, scuba diving, any kind of hunting, and any other activity deemed by the parents and youth staff to present an unacceptable risk.

OVERNIGHT EVENTS

1. Parent permission slip required.
2. "Parent Information Sheet" to be available a week in advance, giving exact destination, emergency phone number, and list of adult staff attending.
3. It is assumed that young people attending overnight events/retreats will not leave the event while it is going on. Exceptions must be specifically added to the parent permission slip.

TRANSPORTATION

1. The church bus and van are driven only by properly licensed and trained persons. All church vehicle drivers will be listed on the church insurance policy.
2. Vehicles will not be overloaded. All those riding the van will wear seat belts.
3. Aisles and emergency exits will be kept clear at all times.
4. Rowdy behavior (for example, wrestling) is not permitted.
5. The driver of the vehicle has final authority to determine what is safe behavior.
6. In socials that require young people to be transported, generally the church bus and/or van will be the assumed mode. Sometimes circumstances require additional transportation and adult drivers will generally be used. If high school age drivers are projected to be necessary, the fact will be noted on the parent copy of the quarterly social calendar.

There are cases that arise where high school age people choose to drive. Parents not wishing their son/daughter to ride in a high school age driver's car should (1) instruct their son/daughter accordingly and (2) inform the youth pastors. It is recognized there still may be instances where young people make transportation choices that do not reflect the wishes of the parents or the youth staff.

WATER

1. Around water where no certified lifeguard is present, an adult will be designated to watch the water for swimmers in trouble or for unsafe behavior.

2. In lakes with no lifeguard: Kids must stay within 15 yards of shore. No one is allowed to swim across any lake.
3. At the ocean: No swimming when the tide is going out. No one goes beyond waist deep water in any case.
4. No jumping off rocks or trees, if higher than 15 feet, and only after an adult has checked the depth and safety of the water below. No diving allowed.
5. Waterskiing or boating: All will wear life jackets. Outboard will be driven by adults and include a spotter as well.

HIKING

1. No off-trail hiking.
2. No one hikes alone.
3. Mines and caves will not be entered.
4. Adult supervision appropriate to the conditions will be provided.
5. It is recognized that on some day hikes part of the group may choose to relax in the sun, while others want to walk around the lake or otherwise explore. Those wishing to do so must be with at least one other person and will be briefed as to the time they need to be back. Parents not wishing their son/daughter to be allowed to leave the main group in such fashion should inform their son/daughter accordingly as well as the Youth Staff person leading the trip.

BACKPACKING

1. No more than twelve kids per trip.
2. All must have "essential" safety equipment specified in the publicity brochure. Equipment will be checked by staff.

MALE/FEMALE

1. Boys and girls are not allowed in each other's rooms or tents. (Exception: When a group meeting/gathering has been called/approved by one of the leaders and designates a certain room or tent as the meeting place.)
2. Boys and girls are not permitted to sleep outside in a mixed group.

STAFFING

1. On overnight trips or events: 1:7 staff to student ratio.

2. On day trips: 1:10 staff to student ratio. When the group is split and a group is larger than seven, an adult will be with each group.
3. "Staff in Training" (college age) may be used, but are not to be a majority of the staff.

EMERGENCY PROCEDURES

1. In the rare cases where the group splits and goes to separate locations, all staff will have been oriented on emergency procedures and how to reach the person in charge of the event.
2. At the beginning of each school year, parents will be provided with a medical services authorization form. Those who wish may sign, have the form notarized, and return it to the church office. These forms will accompany the youth staff on all outings where emergency medical assistance might be required and the parent cannot be notified.

DISCIPLINE OF INAPPROPRIATE BEHAVIOR

The committee feels it neither necessary nor wise to spell out a potentially exhaustive list of misbehaviors and the expected disciplines. The procedures currently being followed will be continued. That is, behavior that includes intentional violation on the part of the young person of stated rules, alcohol, drug, tobacco use, and other forms of unacceptable behavior will be dealt with in a timely manner by the youth staff. Parents will be notified.

Yes, all this may seem about as interesting as reading the book of Leviticus. All I can say, though, is that it has helped us have credibility with some parents who would otherwise be suspicious and miserly in their support of youth group activities.

* * *

To make it in youth ministry, we need to work positively with our senior pastors and with the parents. Let's not forget the kids! Do you enjoy youth ministry and love young people? The kids will *know* the answer to those questions. If the answer to either or both is "no" or "I'm not sure," your future prospects are not encouraging. How can we communicate joy in ministry and love for teenagers?

CHAPTER SEVEN
WORKING POSITIVELY
WITH KIDS

It was a sleepy Saturday morning on the senior high leadership overnight. The meal had been memorable. . . . I made breakfast and it actually turned out to be fit for human consumption. A few in the group even tried my culinary innovation: cheese and chocolate omelettes. Like I said, breakfast was memorable.

I sat on the couch letting my stomach settle and watched as the twelve senior highers played the game "Balderdash" with surprising gusto. The night before, we had prayed for each member of our youth group by name. Combined with praise and worship, it was an evening in which we had nearly touched heaven.

The World War II hero General George Patton surveyed a battle scene and was heard to say something like, "God, I love this." I watched these twelve leadership kids enjoying each other and the time together. "God, I love this," I silently prayed. "I'm doing what I was born to do."

Strangely, not all youth workers like working with kids. I've asked many young people and staff members about their youth pastors. One question I ask is this: "Does your youth pastor love youth ministry and does he or she love kids?" Some of the answers are quite amazing: "No, she cries a lot. She can't stand it when we're rowdy. She hates practical jokes. She withdraws most of the time."

"Definitely not! He's always talking about quitting. He's easily discouraged. He gets depressed a lot, too."

"No, he wants to be a senior pastor. I can tell he doesn't like our church either."

"He's never happy. He likes to make people feel guilty whenever he talks. No way do I bring friends anymore."

Pity the poor young people who are stuck in a group led by a sour youth worker!

To be successful in youth ministry we *must* learn to love kids. If we don't, the party is truly over. Let's look together at young people as we did parents and pastors.

UNDERSTANDING THEM

Part of working positively with young people is understanding them and knowing what constitutes normal kid behavior. Relax—we are not going to rehearse long passages from Piaget, Fowler, and other developmental luminaries from the exciting world of academia. There are some main ideas, however, that we'd better get a grip on. If we don't, we'll feel stomach upset often in youth ministry . . . and it won't be the food that causes it. Take the following quiz to test your knowledge of kid development and its impact on church youth ministry.

1. The reason many twelve- to fifteen-year-old boys are spiritual nerds compared many to twelve- to fifteen-year-old girls is:
   ___a. God is really female and thus she relates better to girls.
   ___b. Girls get the ability to think abstractly before boys.
   ___c. Girls imitate the spirituality of more mature people and boys don't.
2. A decision to recommit their lives to Christ will more likely last when:
   ___a. They are juniors or seniors in high school.
   ___b. It snows in Hawaii.
   ___c.The youth worker is physically attractive.
3. Much of church is boring to junior high school kids because:
   ___a. They want to get home and do their homework.
   ___b. The prayers and sermons are too long and not in their language.
   ___c. The pastor is not a sports megahero.
4. Young people can have a true biblically based self-esteem when:
   ___a. They are mature enough to understand deeply that God cares about them.

___b. They obtain their own copy of the *NIV Study Bible*.

___c. They are better looking than everyone else in the group.

5. When a kid in my youth group questions the existence of God, I:

___a. Call the elders or the pastor.

___b. Thank God he/she is right on schedule.

___c. Pray that he/she will be healed of his/her doubt.

6. The most effective entry ticket into the junior high in-crowd is:

___a. Money.

___b. Parental occupation.

___c. Physical development and attractiveness.

7. When senior highers sit down at the youth group program or on the church bus:

___a. Most of them want to sit close to others who need ministry.

___b. Many of them position themselves close to someone of the opposite sex they want to know better.

___c. The shortest sit in the front, the tallest in the back.

8. To break up cliques in the youth group:

___a. A simple reminder should do the trick.

___b. A series of messages with heavy prayer will do the job.

___c. Cliques will not be broken up, no matter what we do.

9. Kids are *very* aware of their bodies:

___a. Yes.

___b. Definitely.

___c. All of the above.

10. When a kid perceives his/her body to be different from peers:

___a. It's no big deal.

___b. He/she consults a doctor immediately.

___c. This is an issue of immense concern.

11. Early adolescents are physically awkward because:

___a. They're growing fast and they don't know where their ends are.

___b. They are *not* physically awkward; *or*

___c. They like to make the few kids who *are* awkward feel less foolish.

12. Emotionally, kids are generally:

___a. More stable than their parents.

___b. Happy.

___c. Really up or really down.

13. Kids generally appreciate enthusiasm in their leaders:

___a. greatly.

___b. only when they are not sleepy.

___c. only when they drink or do drugs.

14. What seem to us like little problems for kids seem big to them because:

___a. They like to exaggerate.

___b. They don't have enough life experience yet to see their troubles in a wider context.

___c. They are generally shorter than we are.

How do you think you did? Let's look at these by category.

Questions 1-5, Mental Development: Correct Answers:
1 = b, 2 = a, 3 = b, 4 = a, and 5 = b.

In the brain of a young person, something truly amazing happens in adolescence. More mental wires get connected. Previously unused brain capacity arouses itself into life. The Commodore 64 child mind becomes an IBM 486 forty megabyte hard drive wonder. This cerebral upgrade starts occurring in girls first, during ages eleven to fourteen. Most boys, for reasons only God knows, don't get the upgrade until ages fourteen to sixteen.

When it happens, kids who have been raised in the church mentally reinventory everything they've previously learned. It's natural for them to question the existence of God . . . they are in the process of making faith more than a religious hangover from parents. They understand the Gospel's *implications* for their lives. This is why kids who become Christians as young children often rededicate their lives to Christ as teenagers. It's not unusual for them to rededicate several times and it is fine that they do. As their cerebral capacity expands, more and more sectors of their thinking and life get reevaluated in terms of Christ's teachings.

When it comes to self-esteem, most seventh graders won't feel secure unless they look like and have the same things as their peers. When they are eleventh graders, they'll have the capacity to understand that to be okay with the Lord is most important and that the rest is not as crucial as it once was.

Appreciating mental development also helps us have sympathy for the junior high boys who sit in adult church. The language, the length of prayers and speeches, and the sit-still-to-listen format are geared for upgraded minds, not theirs.

Questions 6-8, The Social Agenda of Adolescence:
Correct Answers: 6 = c, 7 = b, and 8 = c.

In elementary school, the social groups consist of exclusively boys or exclusively girls. In junior high, however, some kids begin to explore relationships with the opposite sex. Usually these are the ones most developed physically and socially. Take the lid off of any junior high school and the in-crowd will be a group of guys and girls together. These are the movers and shakers of early adolescent society as the rest look on with envy.

Since one of the purposes of adolescence is to move from dependence to independence, there is a natural transference of some loyalties from the home to the peer group. Kids need each other and they cluster themselves for protection and identification. This intense clustering abates for many in late high school, but until then a clique is a clique is a clique.

Speaking of cliques, in the North Seattle Alliance Church youth group we harness clique power to our advantage. Our group is divided into five teams, each consisting of four or five friendship clusters. When we divide into teams for a game or discussion the kids happily go, because their friends are in the same group. The sneaky part is this—in these teams they actually start interacting with youths outside their friendship cluster and at least a reasonable facsimile of unity develops among the team members as the year goes along. Our youth group draws kids from a 300-square-mile rectangle of Seattle-area real estate, so unity is something that doesn't happen automatically.

Of course, most high schoolers want to enjoy a relationship with the opposite sex. There is an immense amount of socially motivated jockeying that takes place in our youth groups each week. It's fun to watch if we know what to look for.

Questions 9-12, Physical Development:
Correct Answers 9 = c, 10 = c, and 11 = a.

Hormonally triggered growth propels the young person to almost all of his/her adult height by age nineteen. In the fast-growing years, the extremities are getting farther from the brain so rapidly that the central nervous system can't keep track of them. This is why early adolescent boys and girls run into things. Part of the brain sees clearly what's coming, but surprise . . . the foot, the leg, the arm, the shoulder is bigger than it was yesterday, so . . . crash!

Our hearts should go out to young people as they try to maintain their emotional health in view of a body that is going berserk. Walk into any group of young people and you can be sure that each of them is aware of his/her own body, how it compares with others, and how their looks match up to the "10's" they see in magazines and on TV.

Questions 12-14, Emotional Development:
Correct Answers: 12 = c, 13 = a, and 14 = b.

Up and down emotions are normal for a young person. They are experiencing so much of "adult" life for the first time . . . the joys are stellar and the disappointments are catastrophic. Enthusiasm and energy for life is a commodity highly valued by young people. Those who have it find willing followers among those who don't.

As we review and remember what is normal for young people in terms of development, we reduce the stress we feel about kid behavior. It becomes easier to love them as we see their hearts . . . trying to keep their balance in a rapidly changing social environment where the footing has become slick as ice.

INTEGRITY: BEING LIKABLE
WITHOUT BEING FAKE

Ask any young person to describe his or her favorite teacher. What will we hear? We'll hear about men and women who are funny, approachable, enthusiastic, easy to understand, and who seem to genuinely care about their students. What makes a likable schoolteacher also makes a likable youth worker. I've asked dozens of young people in the United States and Canada to write down why they like their youth pastor or how they know he/she loves them personally. Here is some of that feedback:

"He's always there for me and he tells us all that he loves us."

"She is always fun to be around. She's radiant."

"He is involved with my life . . . he comes to my activities at school to support me."

"You can tell she delights in seeing us grow in God."

"This guy's on fire for God and he loves to be with us."

"He treats us like we're his age, not kids. He calls everyone, too."

"He accepts us unconditionally."

"She loves to laugh with us."

Is there a "best personality type" for youth ministry? Certainly God can use anyone if he or she truly loves kids, yet those who are outgoing, caring, positive, and enthusiastic will get a faster start than those who are not.

Kids will instantly notice if we do things beyond what our job requires of us. I like to send notes of encouragement. It's fun to just phone for no reason except to say "Hi" and to see if there are any major prayer requests. In our youth group, if you come down with mononucleosis, you'll get flowers from me if you're a girl, and a toy if you're a boy. The death of the family dog will trigger at least a nice card, if not flowers and a visit.

As youth workers we look for ways to express our care and give it sincerely. If kids see we are sincerely trying to love them, it is hard for them not to think well of us. I pray often that God will continue to increase my love for young people and the joy I have in being with them.

BUILDING BRIDGES

Communication: Getting Beyond Hello. Working positively with kids means we will have good communication with them— talk that is two-way, comfortable, mutually satisfying.

When on my way to a youth group event, I consciously remind myself what world I am entering. It is a world of sports, school pressures, music, movies, cars, and the Lord. Showing a sincere interest in their lives grants me entrance into their conversations. I share my life with them as well; asking for their opinions is appreciated. Recently my parents surprised my wife and me with a $15,000 gift for the purchase of a new car. Of course the youth group heard about it (I told them!!!) and it was great fun gathering their advice on the subject of what car would be best for the money (we got a Ford Taurus wagon).

A few months ago, I phoned most of the youth group members for advice on a schedule change in the youth calendar. Sure, I had the authority to make that decision unilaterally. It was a chance, though, to include kids and thus ascribe to them value and importance.

The Selection, Care, and Feeding of Leadership Youths. Early on in our ministry, we will want to make sure it has a youth leadership base instead of only an adult leadership base. How this is accomplished varies from church to church. The method I use to form a Cabinet (our youth leadership team) is a composite stolen from a variety of youth pastors, and molded to fit our own circumstances. Now I fondly call it "The North Seattle Alliance Church Poll-Screen-Appointment Cabinet Method."

In May, I present the youth group with a list of next year's group. In other words, eighth graders are off the junior high list and twelfth graders are bumped from the senior high list. The list has boys on one side, girls on the other. After prayer, I ask them to circle the names of the peers who best meet the following qualifications: (1) Most committed to Christ; (2) Most committed to the youth group.

Junior highers select six: three boys and three girls; the senior highers choose twelve. I then meet with the outgoing leadership eighth or twelfth grade leaders and we prayerfully compile the list.

We determine a "Plan A" list of kids to approach first, and a "Plan B" list to ask if not all the Plan A people say yes.

Approaching the chosen properly, I've learned, can save a lot of grief later on down the line. If I'm phoning Larry to ask him to be on this leadership team, here is the gist of my speech:

> "Larry, you remember we took that Cabinet poll a couple of weeks ago in youth group, right? Well, I'm happy to let you know that a lot of people in the youth group really see you as a spiritual leader and so do I. We'd very much like to see you on the Senior High Cabinet for next school year.
>
> "You probably already know what this leadership group is for . . . we plan all the events, but more importantly, we try to lead this group spiritually.
>
> "We don't expect leadership people to be perfect. We do expect, though, that leadership people be growing in the Lord and be willing to be held accountable for the growth in devotions and a daily walk with God.
>
> "I know you already know we expect leadership members to have nearly perfect attendance at all Senior High Wednesdays, socials, and Sunday school sessions. To be in the leadership group means you are making the youth group among your highest priorities for the year. This means that if you get a job that eliminates you from attending, you can't be on the Cabinet. The Cabinet meets every other Sunday afternoon at 4:00 p.m., and those meetings are not optional.
>
> "I know you are an excellent basketball player, and will probably make varsity this year. The way we've worked it in the past is that if a leadership person needs to disappear from part of the ministry for one sports season, that is okay. I know you wouldn't be able to come on Wednesdays during

basketball season, right? Well, that's fine. However, if you contemplate being in a second sport in another season that takes you away from the group, that would eliminate you from being on the Cabinet. You can see I am asking you to really consider your use of time next year and to make some decisions.

"Whadayathink? . . ."

We announce the names of the new leadership group the first Sunday in June. We meet monthly during the summer and then twice monthly starting in September. In a typical meeting we . . .

a. Pray for each other (usually this takes thirty minutes).
b. Review the previous two weeks . . . any problems or issues?
c. Preview the coming two weeks . . . and do any longer-range planning that's necessary.
d. Talk about new people, and share how we are doing at connecting with them.
e. Do leadership training.
f. Get on our knees in a circle and pray for the youth group.

It's not hard to see why I look forward to these meetings. It's an incredible privilege to share the ministry with these young people and to see vision grow in their spirits. This leadership group also leads the opening part of our Sunday school, gives testimonies in other groups, and generally practices leadership. These young people are also my eyes and ears in the group if something is wrong.

"Say, Len, I'm glad to be on this retreat and I just wanted to mention that I've brought two bottles of vodka and quite an assortment of drugs to share with my cabin. Yep, we're going to have a wonnnnnderful time!"

Funny thing, no one has ever approached me like that in over twenty years of ministry. However, leadership youth have approached me with similar information about their peers on many occasions.

Working positively with young people is not only good for kids and their leadership development, it's good for us. Youths who care for us too . . . it is not why we are in ministry, but it sure makes up for some of the hassles we must endure.

* * *

Working positively with kids is one of the things we do first and best in youth ministry. Youth workers are famous for their direct ministry with kids. Youth workers are infamous, however, for their management skills or lack thereof.

CHAPTER EIGHT
MANAGEMENT 101

Remember the long lunch I told you about in Chapter Four? A board member who was also on the volunteer youth staff gave me the news over a luncheon steak that I wasn't doing so well. He had my undivided attention.

"Len," he began, "I think you pretty well know what you are doing when it comes to working with kids and that's great. But you've got real problems when it comes to working with adults. Your skills are good at one level, but lacking at another.

"You know, I work with executives all over the world. There is a truth in the business world—an outstanding salesman may get promoted by his or her company to be a sales manager. Some people who get that promotion will completely fail in their new jobs. Why? It takes a whole different set of skills to be a sales manager than to be a salesman. A great sales manager may get promoted and become a regional sales manager. Again, the person may bomb out completely at that level. It takes different skills to manage managers than it does just to be one."

He went on, "In your ministry you have to function at several skill levels. Level I is working with kids and Level II is being organized yourself. I'll give you high marks there. Level III is working with adults who want to work with kids . . . like me. You've succeeded in frustrating all of us at this level during the year. Level IV is when you set up coordinating people who help you work with the adult volunteers. It takes different skills to work with them. I think you can work to improve so you can function at more than just the first or second levels."

Lee gave me a lot to think about: four sets of skills were needed to succeed in local church youth ministry. Lack of organization is the downfall of many youth pastors . . . 20 percent of those who get fired do so because of incompetence in this area. In this chapter, we'll tour Levels I and II. In the next, we'll move on to Levels III and IV.

LEVEL I SKILLS: WORKING WITH KIDS

Interpersonal Skills. If the youths don't like us, it is not easy to minister to them. In much of youth ministry today, for better or worse, we have to earn the right to lead, be heard, and even to discipline. This skill is so crucial it deserved a chapter all its own.

I received a letter from one of our interns after he finished his year of service. Jack was on the quiet side and was working toward a Ph.D. in philosophy. Because he genuinely loved the senior highers with whom he worked, had more patience than most, and had a healthy ability to laugh at himself, he had a very effective year. Jack wrote, "I formerly held to the primacy of ideas in all areas of life. I can see now, and this is an astounding revelation to me (though, I suppose it is elementary to everyone else), that in youth ministry, relationships are of primary importance, not ideas. In fact, without relationships, correct ideas are seldom received."

Way to go, Jack!

Strong Up-Front Skills. William stood in front of 100 excited junior highers at the first session of the great "Mini-November Getaway." His opening speech went like this. With a sad and serious look on his face he said, "On this retreat we are not going to have any fun. The sessions are going to be boring, and the activities are going to be a drag. If you came to this thing thinking you were going to have fun, you're wrong."

He elaborated on this in some detail, as the expressions on the faces of the junior highers went from smiles to stress-contoured concern.

William was trying to be funny in this opening speech. He had a dry sense of humor and he was trying to be sarcastic. What he meant was that it was going to be an *awesome* retreat. Unfortunately, the junior highers were not tuned in to his wavelength. They didn't catch his sophisticated, subtle humour. He was an adult and was in charge of the retreat. They were getting, as far as they knew, an introduction to how things were going to be.

It took till nearly the last couple hours of the retreat for William to climb out of the hole he had dug for himself in the opening fifteen minutes.

If we are going to work with kids, we must stand up front and lead. Kids like enthusiasm, warmth, positiveness, humor, and certainty. Can we laugh at ourselves? All the better. The stellar personality of a late-night TV show host isn't necessary, but we must be able to lead, somehow.

Are you good enough up front? Want to improve? Try this. Ask a friend to videotape your up-front leadership and teaching. When you watch the tape later, *turn off the sound*. Ask yourself: Do I look like I'm enjoying what I'm doing? Am I confident? Do I project warmth and enthusiasm?

If this little experiment sounds too weird, consider the following: This is exactly how the best media consultants work with presidential candidates as they prepare them for the campaign trail. Most of personal communication is nonverbal. If our body language isn't good enough, what we say will never be given credence. Furthermore, when we meet someone new or stand up in front of a group, *we have no more than seven seconds* before our audience makes up its mind about us. That first impression is very hard to change.[1] Need more convincing? Watch Donahue, Oprah, or Letterman with the sound turned off. Or watch TV commercials that way. How much do they communicate nonverbally?

Administration of Youths. Although personal preparation involves getting ourselves ready in youth ministry, administration means getting others ready. At Level I, the issue is our ability to work with and through young people.

Planning in youth ministry separates the men from the boys. This is a premier Level I skill. *Planning* is simply making plans for the future; *programming* is having those plans actually work out into some eventual activity. Although I believe programming is a Level II skill, planning is Level I when we do it with young people.

It is hard to overestimate the importance of planning in youth ministry. The average person in the pew cares little about the philosophy of ministry we might have. They do care that "something is being done with our young people." That something usually means social or service events, studies, or youth programs. One of the best ways to lose the confidence of the people in your church and shorten your ministry is to fail at planning and then at programming.

For me, short-range planning is two to six months in advance. I do this with the youth leadership for socials and service projects.[2] In June, we plan for September through December. In October, we work on January to March. When January comes, we plan April and May. In March, we plan June to August. This short-range planning is accomplished in four steps.

A. I come to the meeting with a calendar of the weekend dates for the period we are planning. Entered on the calendar are things that we've already scheduled (for example, retreats) and major church activities (for example, the missions conference). I circle the dates (usually one each weekend) that are free on my own schedule to have an event.

B. We brainstorm the things we would like to do . . . trying to come up with a large list. If we run short of ideas, I come up with some based on my reading of *Ideas* or things I've stolen from other youth groups.

C. We fill in the calendar, plugging events into the dates from our list of ideas.

D. We then ask questions: Is it balanced? Are there things here that will interest most members of the youth group? Are there both free and cost events?

I work with the Cabinet to determine our service projects as well. Every six weeks, instead of a normal Wednesday night, we have Reach Out Ministries. In advance, the Cabinet selects four service projects from which those attending the event may choose. A typical menu might be as follows: (a) visitation to the Cerebral Palsy Center; (b) baking cookies in the church kitchen to take to elderly people in the church as thanks for their years of service; (c) visitation to kids who haven't come for a while; or (d) writing letters to youth group graduates who are away at college or in the military. (See Appendix B for sample calendars and schedules.)

Creativity in Bible Teaching. The media mold the way our young people prefer to receive input. They like it short, interesting, varied, and visually appealing. We can bemoan this fact, pray against it, preach against it, or ignore it. We can do whatever we want, but the fact doesn't change. This is not to say that we spoon-feed them spiritual milk only. Christian teenagers want to be challenged.

> *"Ken got fired because his teaching was boring. He couldn't get down to the kids' level. He was a nice guy and everything, but we needed someone who could teach, too. For example, we asked him to do a lesson on historical proof of Jesus. Instead, he gave a philosophy lesson about knowledge in general, and concluded that wanting proof that Jesus ever walked on earth was wrong."*

Helps and seminars abound for us if we want to improve our Bible teaching skills. The resource that has most helped me is Larry Richards' *Creative Bible Teaching.*[3] "Hook-Book-Look-Took" comes naturally now after doing it so much.

Discipleship. Youth workers who end up lasting beyond a couple of years learn a major ministry truth: *Programs don't bring people nearly as well as people bring people.* We can run the flashiest, hippest, most with-it, and exciting programs and we may succeed in wowing the masses for a while. It won't succeed for the long haul, however, because if that's all we give kids they'll get bored with our flash.

A corollary to the first truth is this: *No matter how flashy the program, no matter how winsome the personnel in leadership, kids will, in time, get bored with our ministries* **unless we give them something to do.**

A ministry that has a discipleship focus may still have great programs and personnel, but the focus is on empowering young people with a vision to grow themselves as Christians. It also focuses on empowering young people in ministry to their peers. In a discipling ministry, the leaders consciously pour themselves into the young people. The junior or senior high school kids are then given real responsibility, entrusted with personal or program ministries.

In Chapter Seven I talked about working with the youth leadership in my own church. Additionally, we have discipleship groups in two different formats. Once a quarter we open up an introductory discipleship group to no more than seven kids. It meets on Saturday mornings for eight weeks and has two main foci: (1) being accountable for our walk with God and (2) learning how to disciple someone else. Another format we use is that our female staffers each meet weekly with three girls. Their foci are growth, accountability, and ministry training.

LEVEL II: PERSONAL BALANCE AND SELF-ORGANIZATION

Relaxing in God's Power. How does our spiritual life function? Is my walk with God characterized by rest or effort? Am I letting God's power, through the Holy Spirit, work in my life, or am I still "trying my best to live a good Christian life?" When crunch and crises occur, what happens to my interior life?

We can, as youth workers, have a quality walk with God, sensing his presence and power on a daily basis. This is the skeleton around which our life and ministry are fleshed out.

Aside from Scripture, the book that has influenced me the most is *The Normal Christian Life* by Watchman Nee.[4] One of his main points is that God isn't nearly so much interested to help us as he is interested to do it all, if we learn what it means to lay aside our own strength and self-effort. As we admit our own weaknesses and inadequacies, then we are ready to be filled and infused with that divine dynamite.

Self-Administration: The List. I live by the weekly "List of Things To Do." On Monday morning I write down everything I should accomplish during the week: desk work, phone calls, personal appointments. The desk work list always has a few *very* short-term items. Planning a game for Wednesday night, writing "Youth Scene" bulletin copy, and preparing for Sunday school are examples. There are always some longer-term items as well. In January, for example, I try to get the summer calendar 75 percent done.

January is the time to draft the September schedule and make facility reservations for the winter retreat that will take place fourteen months later.

Looking at the list, I prioritize the items: first, second, third, and so on. Then . . . with much internal fanfare, *I draw the line.* Say what? I look at the list, look at what else is happening during the week, and draw a line on the list. Out of a list of fifteen items, for example, I might draw the line after item twelve. Or, if the week is a heavy one with meetings and appointments, the line might be drawn at eight.

What it means is this: *I will make almost any sacrifice to finish every item above the line. I tell myself that the kingdom of God and his church on earth will probably collapse if I don't finish that list above the line.* Sometimes it has meant my coming back to the office late at night after my children are in bed and working until midnight. It has meant coming in at 6:30 a.m. Once I've drawn the line, it means these items, short of my being sick or dead, will get done. Usually the list above the line gets done without resorting to heroics, but if unexpected time gobblers slide into my week, working on "The List" takes place at odd hours.

The secret of being organized and getting things done for me has been always to include several longer-range items above the line. The first week of January, I may put "order summer Sunday school curriculum" above the line. Sure, it's not really crucial—it could even be done in May. But I try to schedule these things way out in advance, so I never have to scramble at the end.

Have I always been like this? Of course not! Take the little item of "recruit adult staff," for example.

I used to hate it. If there were ever a prize given to the Procrastinator of the World, I would have received at least a nomination. I had elevated putting off recruiting adult staff to an art form. If the slightest addition to my weekly list of things to do occurred, it was with joy and gladness that the "recruit staff" item was bumped to the following week, and the next, and the next. Each week went by until the absolute, final, and unavoidable deadline had arrived. Have you ever tried to recruit Sunday school teachers five days before the start of a new quarter? For the recruiter and the recruitee, it is not exactly an experience in which the joy of the Lord is overflowing.

Sure, I felt guilty and stressed about this. Did I change? No, until . . . I had an experience that was so humiliating, so shameful, so utterly and thoroughly unprofessional, I vowed never to allow it to happen again.

"Adult Christian Ed" had been on my job description for a year. For several months, I had in mind to ask Al to teach Sunday school beginning in the fall term. He was on top of the pile in terms of rapport and communication skills. There was no doubt he would succeed if he took the class. As usual, I let the weeks slip by until the approaching September kickoff Sunday was *nine days away.* The secretary who was in charge of the Sunday bulletin wanted the list of classes and teachers for the coming Sunday, and she wanted it today. I confidently phoned Al. No answer. I tried again an hour later. Still no answer. It was the same story two hours after that. I phoned his best friend and found, to my utter horror, that he and his family were on vacation in Idaho and were due back in nine days. As I pondered my options, there were a few moments in which I wondered if perhaps I should have been a forest ranger after all. My situation was especially desperate because I had already approached all my other options and was using them with other classes. My number one choice for this class was, in fact, my only choice.

So, I made the decision that changed my ministry with respect to procrastination. I decided to track this person down on his vacation. A few sweaty phone calls later, I had Al on the other end of the line at a motel in Idaho. He and his family were enjoying a restful and carefree vacation, and here I was almost begging him to teach Sunday school—and to start in nine days. Mercifully, he said yes. My mental health had been spared! This experience was so traumatic and embarrassing, I had to face my failure squarely and vow in my heart to change.

Making the list and drawing the line has cured me of procrastination. On Monday I begin working on item number one, and throughout the week whenever I am at my desk, I pick up where I left off. Some weeks I get beyond the line, but not many.

I can't claim my approach to "The List and The Line" is inspired, but to be successful in ministry we have to have some method by which we get things done.

Controlling Paper. Similarly, if were going to make it in youth ministry we have to figure out how to control paper.

Have you ever wanted to rent a bulldozer or backhoe to clean off the top of your desk? I sure have. Oh, how nice it would be just to scoop it all up and spill it out the window to an eager dumpster below.

I like files and notebooks. My senior high Cabinet notebook has the following sections: Cabinet meetings: future, current, and past; Team lists; Planning calendar; and Ideas. My senior high group section in the file cabinet includes such files as Current Quarter Wednesdays; Socials: pending, current, and past; Retreats: pending, current, and past; Reach Out Ministries; Parent meetings: pending, current, and past; and Discipleship.

For the Bible, I have one hanging file folder for every book. This is especially helpful since our junior and senior highers are on a six-year curriculum plan (see Appendix C). The junior highers repeat every two years and the senior highers every four. Since I have been at this church thirteen years, I am now on my fourth time through the cycle with the senior highers. We're due to look at 1 Timothy next quarter. When the time comes, I'll just go to my 1 Timothy file and see what I've done four, eight, and twelve years ago. Some of the talks I'll totally revamp; others will be used just as they are.

I have a file drawer of other topics: suicide, sex, peer pressure, and so on. Another drawer has information from youth organizations: Youth Specialties, SonLife, Group, Youth For Christ, and so on.

It doesn't matter how we do it, but we have to do it successfully—manage the paper we create and manage the paper that comes our direction. It's not hard to see how success here helps us in long-term ministry. If the Cabinet wants to do a van rally, we don't have to start from zero. I can go to my "Socials: Past" file. It is further subdivided so I have a separate file on van rallies, scavenger hunts, and similar socials. We can choose a van rally that was done more than four years ago. We pull the paper on it, revise it if we want, and go to press.

Personal Preparation. Preparation style is an intensely personal and individual matter, but the bottom line is not. When we come to something for which we have responsibility, are we ready? Have we worked hard or do we wing it hard? Have we avoided the "Saturday Night Special Syndrome"? I encourage youth workers to avoid last-minute preparation because Murphy's Law is alive and well—if something can go wrong, it probably will. When things that are prepared in advance come apart, at least we have time to glue them back together.

One time when I was just getting started in youth ministry, I finished my Wednesday night preparation at home late that afternoon. I zoomed into the church parking lot five minutes prior to the start of the meeting that I was supposed to lead. Crucial to the evening were some photocopied small-group instructions. As I opened the church office door, I could see through the dim twilight filtering into the room that there was a sign on the photocopy machine. As I approached, my heart sank as I read the words: "Machine broken, repairman coming tomorrow morning." Oh well, I scrambled to come up with a Plan B.

✳ ✳ ✳

Level I and II skills are crucial to functioning as a youth worker. Let's now look at Level III and Level IV skills. If we get our act together here, they'll rise up and call us blessed.

CHAPTER NINE

MANAGEMENT 102

Moving from Levels I and II to Level III is like the transition from grade school to junior high. In grade school there is one teacher, one desk, one group of classmates, and a predictable routine with easily understood expectations. Remember the confusion of junior high on day one? Six or seven classes and teachers, a big unfamiliar building, and no desk to call your very own. From the pinnacle of grade school social prestige and power, we tumbled into the abysmal bottom of junior high society. As early adolescent lowlifes, we were left to ricochet among coagulating friendship clusters until one would let us stick.

Working with youth sponsors can be just as confusing. By the time I had reached my second "full-time" youth ministry position, I figured out there were some advantages in having other people assist. I did not bother to write my expectations down, I just recruited people to be youth sponsors. They showed up at events, assisted where needed, and built relationships with kids. Because I was intimidated by persons older than myself, the youth staff consisted of persons my age and younger. When I wasn't present they took over as best they knew how. We had no scheduled meetings, communication was irregular, and though we got along well, few continued to serve beyond one school year. Some quit before the year was up.

I didn't know it, but this was ministry at Level III and I was a rookie. I felt like a lower life form. Trying to work with adults was very intimidating.

Working at Level III means we are managing people. We are working with and through other adults toward the accomplishment of the same purpose. To get help in this area I read several books on leadership and several more on management. Some were Christian, others were secular. I even went to three management seminars. I closely watched people who were good leaders. With a little effort anyone can sharpen his or her leadership skills. Many resources are available, some of which are listed at the conclusion of this chapter.

Here are some skills that are basic to functioning at Level III in youth ministry.

LEVEL III:
WORKING THROUGH ADULTS

Visualizing. Can we visualize exactly and in good detail what we want our youth staff to do? What, *really*, do we want them to do? Everyone likes to feel successful, right? How will they know when they are succeeding?

Once we have it in our mind, we need to write it down. I like to write job descriptions. It helps me clarify in my own mind what I want done, and it helps our staff members know what is expected of them without much ambiguity. Here is a sample of one of the youth ministry job descriptions I use.

Senior High Ministry Team Member

A. FUNCTION

To be used by the Lord in the lives of senior high young people. To love, encourage, and become closely involved with them. To do everything possible to make North Seattle Alliance Church's ministry with senior high school kids excellent.

B. RESPONSIBILITIES

1. *For Your Ministry*
   a. To attend senior high Wednesday night ministries. To attend senior high socials on a rotating basis (at least once every four to six weeks).
   b. To build relationships with the senior high school kids on your team, working closely with the team leaders.
   c. To phone or have personal contacts with people in your team during the year.
   d. To help lead your team in the context of the Wednesday ministry.

2. *For Your Own Growth*
   a. To have a consistent and quality devotional life, growing more and more in love with him.
   b. To attend ministry team meetings, usually twice quarterly.
   c. To listen to one tape or read one book on youth ministry during the year.
3. *You'll Know You Are Succeeding When:*
   a. You know the names of the youth group members and something about them.
   b. You feel comfortable talking with them informally.
   c. You can lead a discussion or prayer time with your team during the Wednesday night ministry.
   d. Kids come up to you to say "Hi" or to talk.
   e. You know them well enough so they feel free to talk with you about personal problems or spiritual topics.
   f. You have a sense of shared ministry with your team leaders.
   g. You occasionally carve out time for personal ministry with your team members outside of the regular youth group meeting times.

C. TERM OF SERVICE

One school year. Everyone is "fired" in June, but welcome to sign up for the next school year. You are expected to take the summer off from youth ministry, since summer staff is recruited to work from June through August. If special circumstances warrant, you may join the summer staff.

It's not easy to have the Level III skill of visualizing if we are just starting out in ministry. We haven't been around the calendar track enough times to know what needs to be done. In this case, the best advice is to steal like a bandit. Look at ministries you respect; study their job descriptions; mold them to your own tastes.

Communication and Follow-Through. Visualizing is pointless unless we can communicate. Once we have in mind what needs to be done, we can begin to get our ideas across to others. We can't assume that just because we've written it down it will be understood.

Every year I try to start something in the ministry that I've never done before. I look for something that is a risk, that stretches my faith, and that keeps me on my knees trusting in God's power.

In my third year of ministry here, a bold plan was conceived in my ever-churning mind: We would have the junior highers lead the opening of their meetings. They would do the first thirty minutes with crowd breakers, games, and announcements, and I would do the teaching and the wrap-up. What's so avant-garde about that? I decided to do this through one of the junior high adult staff . . . equipping him and turning him loose to recruit kids and work with them.

I wrote a prize-winning job description, had a couple of long lunches with James, and was fully convinced this innovation would be nothing short of spectacular. By the end of April, I thought James was trained and ready to begin preparations. The new thrust was to begin in September.

Confident of James's ability, I waited until only a few days before our first September junior high meeting to give him a call regarding his progress. "Yeah, Len, things are going great. I've got the follow-up pretty well figured out and the kids will be good in their leadership of the small groups at the end of your talks."

My heart sank . . . he was working toward almost the exact opposite of what I had "clearly" asked him to do. Well, at least it had been clear in my mind. Since he had given this so much time and work we proceeded as he envisioned. As I feared, the first night bombed and bombed badly. The kids whom James had recruited to be small group leaders were not able to get their peers to take them seriously. The small group time became a joke.

I think James understood what I wanted in April. However, sometime afterward he lost the job description, didn't think about it again until August, and had a very leaky memory when he finally began to work on it.

This is not the only time I've been faced with my shortcomings in communication and follow-through. My first step in improvement came with the publication of printed quarterly schedules for our Wednesday, Sunday, and event ministries. The Wednesday schedule gives the dates, text or topic, who's leading the opening, who's teaching, and who's closing the meeting. Sundays are similarly laid out (see Appendix B).

According to our ministry team members, the most helpful piece of paper I've ever produced is the "Who's Doing What Flow Sheet" for our youth events. Prepared quarterly, it lays out the details of the socials the Cabinet has planned. It includes the date, time, name of event, who's in charge, what extra staff are committed to go, and how the event will be publicized.

We meet as a staff every four weeks to go over all that has been planned. Every month staff members receive a "Leadership Letter" that also reviews what is coming up. Additionally, all staff receive the "When the Buck Stops with You" summary sheet. It generically reviews what they have to consider when they're in charge of an event: how to schedule the use of rooms in the church, the bus, video equipment, how to handle the money, and so on.

Sure, it may seem like a lot of paperwork, but once this stuff started happening two changes occurred: miscues stopped, and no one complained that he or she didn't know what was going on.

Scheduling. When there are other adult staff members to consider, planning and scheduling cannot be done on the spur of the moment. If we expect adult volunteers to be present, we have to get ministry events on their calendars before anything else.

When our senior high leadership plans April to June events in January, the schedules are ready for review at the February ministry team meeting. We all come with our own personal calendars and we divide the event responsibilities as evenly as we can.

Motivating. Our staff members will look to us for inspiration and encouragement in ministry. They will take their cues from our example and our enthusiasm. Also, we must care for and affirm those who work with us. Kenneth Blanchard, author of *The One Minute Manager*,[1] exhorts us to find someone doing good and praise him or her for it. If this is good advice on the assembly line or in the brokerage house, it is good advice in youth ministry.

Of course, people work for the Lord, not for us, yet it does not hurt to tell people we like what they do. Even the apostle Paul was good at this: "I thank my God every time I remember you" (Phil. 1:3).

If we are to last beyond the opening months of ministry, we need regular meetings with our volunteer staff that serve not just to inform, but also to affirm and equip. A typical agenda for our youth group staff follows this pattern:

- Dessert or dinner together.
- Sharing and prayer for each other (half the meeting is often spent doing this).
- A training presentation (about fifteen minutes).
- Review of past month: How'd we do?
- Preview of coming month: Who's doing what?
- Discussion of individual kids, problem situations, and concerns.
- Pray for the ministry.
- Hot tub time (if possible).

All of us on the youth staff look forward to these meetings . . . they are not just business sessions . . . they serve to encourage and support us as fellow travelers in the Christian life.

Time Frame Expansion.[2] Here is a one-question survey. Go ahead, think about it, and write your answer in the space provided.

*When it comes to detailed advanced planning, how far ahead are you comfortable working?*_____

It doesn't take much effort to observe that people have vastly different abilities when it comes to thinking ahead. Some folks have trouble just figuring out what they are going to do today and in what order. Ask them to think about next month and their brain experiences cerebral gridlock. Others, to the amazement of the rest of us, can comfortably work on a project that is three years ahead as if it were only three weeks away. They can see into the future to the expected result, confidently work backward in their mind to the present, and anticipate what needs to be done at each step of the way.

Welcome to the world of how executives think. From the hallowed halls of business academia comes research that reveals good executives actually think differently than normal people. The chief difference is something called "time frame expansion." The good executive has more than pie-in-the-sky vision . . . he or she can comfortably see and correctly sequence the steps necessary to get to the future.

Like it our not, once our youth staff gets beyond one in number, we are executives. We are managing people. Simply put—to function in youth ministry we need to comfortably learn to think ahead.

Ability to think ahead can increase with age. We are capable of progressing from a one-day time frame, to a week, then to a month, then to a quarter, half year, year, two years, and beyond. The research shows, however, that "time frame ability" is distributed like a pyramid.[3] Only one person in several million is capable of a twenty-year time frame. The vast majority of people are never able to think beyond three months.

This information is dynamite for the youth leader. Most young people have only a one-day or a one-week time frame; even most adults seldom think beyond one to two months. *To make youth ministry work, we must learn to be at least one step ahead of the people we work with.*

When I recruit adults for anything, I *always* try to do so at least three months in advance. The reason? I can be almost certain that they don't think that far ahead. Saying yes to my proposal sounds easy since it sounds so far away. If they say yes, their commitment to me takes priority when other decisions about time use are made later. Here, our prime recruiting months for fall ministries are April and May. I try to have the whole school year's staffing needs met by the previous June first.

When we move to a new church and/or are starting out in ministry, a *three-month time frame* is the *absolute minimum* we need. Very rapidly we then need to progress to six- and twelve-month time frames. We learn very quickly that we can't expect to schedule summer retreat facilities in May.

What should our time frame goal be? Eighteen months is about right, though two to three years is even better. An eighteen-month time frame gives us the ability to envision the whole coming school year in March or April. Relax . . . most youth pastors won't be able to do this until they have been in ministry at least a couple of years.

One tool I frequently use in ministry is a planning flow sheet. It illustrates how an expanded time frame works.

SENIOR HIGH OUTREACH SKI RETREAT
APRIL 5-7, 1991

GOAL (broad statement of overall success): A great retreat that helps our senior highers win some friends to Christ.

MEASURE (specific definition of what success will look like):
1. At least sixty senior highers present, at least ten of whom are not Christians.
2. Four make first-time decisions for Christ.
3. Don't lose any money.

STEPS (with deadlines):

1. Sign contract on facility rental.	5/89
2. Finalize speaker and music.	5/90
3. Determine staff coordinators for:	10/90
a. food	
b. program	
c. transportation	
d. promotion	
e. equipment	
f. staff	
4. Determine budget.	10/90
5. Promotion:	
a. make and print brochure	11/90
b. send to kids	1/91 and 3/91
c. phone follow-up	3/91
6. Program:	
a. first draft	10/90
b. discuss with Cabinet	11/90
c. exact and final copy	1/91
d. staff mailing with schedule	3/91
e. mailing to parents of attendees with staff list, emergency numbers, and so on	3/91

Charting out programs in advance like this has many advantages. It helps us avoid the wild-eyed-youth-worker syndrome . . . rushing around like chickens with our heads cut off. It is excellent for delegating. Doing a schedule like this forces me to think things through in exquisite detail. Most importantly, it precludes barriers to spiritual results.

Time frame expansion is a vital Level III skill. Do this well, and your ministry will never be criticized for lack of direction.

Ministry at Level III—if we're good at it, they'll rise up and call us blessed. If we're not, people will be frustrated and we may lose our jobs. From my file of firings, consider these sample cases. The names have been changed, of course:

Diane, twenty-four, served at her church for five years before she was fired. The kids loved her, but she never was able to successfully work with adults. She recruited college-age people to help in the youth ministry and this caused increasing frustration on the part of parents. She had trouble with long-range planning; the end came on a missions trip to Mexico that never left the church parking lot. The parents called a halt to the project only a few days before departure because their questions about where the kids would stay and what they would specifically be doing were not answered with sufficient clarity.

Richard, twenty-nine, served his church for only two years. The group had exploded in numerical growth after his first few months of ministry. Richard, a master at big programs, proved to be inept at handling the administration of a large group. It all fell apart during his second year. There was not enough staff. What staff he did have became frustrated because they never knew what was happening. Event information was often late or inadequate. Kids felt there was no one they could talk to.

Peter, twenty-eight, was fired at the end of two years. Lack of ability in working with sponsors was the reason his pastor gave for the firing. No communication, no affirmation, little organization. He was a master at taking people for granted. It hurt people when he would ask someone to do a task, and then he would do it himself.

Failure at Level III may mean failure to stay employed . . . no doubt about it!

GRADUATING TO THE BIG TIME: LEVEL IV

Moving from Level III to Level IV is like the transition from junior high to high school. Although it is a transition, moving into high school is eagerly anticipated by most. More fun, more opportunities, more freedom.

Level IV ministry holds similar potential. Here we are working with people whom we ask to supervise other volunteers in their ministry with young people.

I enjoy working with Level IV people. Tom coaches our Bible Quiz Team. He has two other adults who assist him in this ministry. Mary is our Senior High Ministry Team Coordinator. She arranges the meetings we have, follows up on those who miss a meeting, and loves to organize others to help in our parent seminars. Nathan organizes our "Reach Out Ministries." Every six weeks, on a Wednesday night, the kids have four service-oriented options to choose from for the evening. Nathan makes sure each of the four is fully staffed and functions well.

Level IV leaders have a deep commitment to what they do. They think about the ministry in the shower, while driving to work, or while jogging. To lead the kids successfully, we need several skills beyond Level III.

Because these people think about the ministry so much, we need the skills of evaluation and flexibility. They will want to assess how things are going and they will want to make improvements. If we jealously maintain the status quo, it will not play well with these people.

Long-range planning and vision are also Level IV skills. In the spring, these folks start coming to me to talk about the needs for the coming school year. To lead them, I need to have thought about it first. Especially our Level IV leaders look to me for vision. What is the larger picture? What is my heart for the ministry? What do I sense God placing on my own heart as I ponder the future of this ministry?

Getting our act together at Levels I, II, and III easily occupies our full attention in the first couple of years. In time, though, we'll know the needs and the people well enough to move to Level IV. This doesn't mean we quit working directly with kids or the youth staff! It only means we have additional leadership help. This "I'll-share-the-load-with-you" help gives us more time to maximize our strengths and shore up our weaknesses in youth ministry.

* * *

We've talked about building fences against failure in our work with the senior pastor, the parents, and the young people. We've looked at management skills we need to make youth ministry work. Some youth workers leave their ministry not because of problems in any of these, but because of moral failure. How do we avoid the twin seductions of money and sex?

CHAPTER TEN

AVOIDING SEDUCTION

The congregation sat in stunned silence as their beloved youth pastor of eight years read the following confession.

"For almost six years I have been stealing from the general offerings of this church. I have taken cash and checks and deposited them into the youth checking account. I then wrote checks for cash on that account and used the money for personal use. I have lied to many of you and have deceived you. The depth of the deception is so ingrained, I do not know the scope of the amount of my stealing. I am dependent upon the elders and their audit to know the scope of my sin.

"Further, I have not filed federal or state income tax for eight years. . . .

"Mine are the sins of stealing, lying, and deceit. Those are the symptoms of a deeper sin of a lack of trusting God and a lack of inner discipline. . . .

"I will be meeting with the district attorney and giving a full confession of my crime.

"In reading this confession, I hereby resign from all pastoral positions and responsibility. I submit to the authority of the elders and to the civil authorities of this nation for God's discipline through them."[1]

A later audit showed that Pastor Alan had embezzled $41,857.35 from the church during the previous six years of ministry. He later served a brief prison sentence, and is slowly making restitution to the church.

As a result of this catastrophe, the leadership of the Euzoa Bible Church in Steamboat Springs, Colorado, made several changes in the church's financial system: (1) they left the offering plates on the communion table during the service instead of storing them in a locked room to await counting, (2) they began a policy of having two people present whenever this money was handled and they made two copies of the counting sheet—one for the deposit bag and one for the financial secretary, and (3) all separate church checking accounts were brought under the general accounting structure of the church. They are balanced monthly by the treasurer and audited annually.

Though many youth workers feel financial pressures, there are several things we can do to build fences against this sort of failure. Taking time to be responsible with money may seem unimportant compared to the megatasks of working at Levels I and II and pleasing parents, kids, and pastors. A mistake here, though, can send us packing, or even to jail.

HAND IN THE TILL

We saw in Chapter Four that the twin seductions of money and sex are a problem for some youth workers as well as pastors. We'll begin with money. As youth workers, we actually count and handle a lot of money directly . . . probably much more than our senior pastors.

Insisting on accountability is one fence we can build against failure. If there is a separate youth group checking account, we should submit it monthly to the church treasurer for balancing and annually for auditing. It's amazing how this simple step forces us to be scrupulous with youth group funds. Better yet, have all youth group funds travel directly through the normal church financial system. It may take a little more paperwork to get money when the youth group needs it, but it thoroughly discourages embezzlement.

Even if we have high personal integrity when it comes to handling youth group money, it is easy to become careless. Church treasurers appreciate receipts, financial summary statements, and other paper trails we are able to provide. Yes, it is paperwork and a bother, but it is essential if we want to keep our name above reproach. Do we keep youth group cash in our top desk drawer? It's an invitation to "borrowing" in a time of need. When it comes to money, our minds easily become leaky about payback.

The basis for good management of youth group money is good management of our own money. Discipline, budgeting, and careful records are a sign of personal maturity. If we are having problems with our own finances, we need to get help immediately.

Reviewing our spending and savings plan with a trusted advisor will help us. I know one youth pastor who commonly runs out of money before he runs out of month. He and his wife go for a few days with only one meal a day, while his two young children get by with only the barest minimum, too. Yet, they faithfully pay for cable TV and carry heavy credit card debt.   But less than 5 percent of the firings I studied were due to money difficulties. Much more prevalent (15 percent) was sexual impropriety.

SEX

I am a library volunteer at Shorecrest High School. Don't laugh! Yes, I know some of my youth pastor friends are athletes and former sports heroes. They love to build bridges with kids by helping coach football or soccer. That's just not me . . . when I was a teenager, my entire sports career lasted four days. It was eighth grade and I tried out for football. I was very confused . . . everyone else seemed to know how to put on his equipment, what position he was playing, and what the coach meant when he used terms like *flanker, set back,* and *flare out.* After four days of torture, the shame was too much for my early adolescent mind to bear and I quit.

Anyway, I get on campus not with my impressive athletic resume, but with my willingness to do grunt labor for the librarians. (By the way, the kids in the youth group love seeing me there. They think it's the funniest thing and they love to bring their friends in to meet me.) I was sitting at the front desk one sleepy Friday morning and I looked up at the social studies class. They were busily checking the card file for important information and quietly working in groups for the next class presentation. Surveying that scene, I sighed and thought to myself, "You know, Len, the girls you see in front of you are as mature and good looking as any of the girls you saw at the University of Washington twenty years ago."

Face it. If you're a guy, you think some of the girls in your youth group are gorgeous, right? When they throw their arms around you, it makes you feel good . . . even cool, right? Recently I was visiting at Shorecrest's rival school and one of the girls from our youth group saw me enter the courtyard. She yelled, "Len!" ran through a crowd of 100 students (who were now watching), and threw her arms around my neck nearly knocking me over.

Of course, my heart rate did not quicken and I felt no pleasure in being greeted so warmly. Ha! Guess again.

Physical attraction seems to have no age barriers when it comes to us males in youth work. One of my best friends in youth ministry, who's just turned fifty, confessed with a chuckle, "Sure, I'm still attracted to the girls in my group, but I know I'm getting old because I'm attracted to their *mothers*, too."

If you're a single female youth worker, especially if you're under thirty, you think some of the boys in your youth group are gorgeous too, right? You really like it when they show kindness to you, and they make you feel special. When standing face-to-face with you they put their hands on your shoulders . . . you look up into their blue eyes and it feels so good when they say, "Ann, I'm so glad you are here." You like it when they offer a back rub on the church bus after a long day of skiing.

Attraction. Is it wrong? I don't think so, at least I hope not. If, from age twelve until now, I had a dollar for every time I felt attraction to someone of the opposite sex, I would be a very wealthy man. Attraction is part of the capabilities God wired into us. Granted, some he seems to have wired with more desire than others, but we all feel it. Attraction is not wrong, but what we do with the feelings may be. Some youth workers handle the attraction feelings well, others don't.

Mark headed back to his office in the "youth house" after the beach trip. It had been an awesome day. Two minutes later there was a knock at his door. Shelley let herself in and closed the door behind her. Shelley was a "ten" if there ever was one, and she was still wearing her bikini. "Mark," she breathed, "would you please give me a back rub?" Alarms started going off in Mark's brain. He stood up, got by her without touching her, and literally ran over to the main church building. Finding his senior pastor he said, "Could my office be moved right next to yours?"[2]

Lynn and her youth pastor husband, Jerry, both worked with the high school group. He wasn't very understanding of her, and their marriage was deteriorating. Lynn had sexual relations with two of the males in the youth group and eventually ran off with one of them. Jerry then had an affair with one of his interns.[3]

Some youth workers deal with the issue of attraction without letting it ruin their ministries or their marriages. It's important to realize that most of the youth workers who let attraction destroy them don't set out to self-destruct.

They don't graduate from Bible college, get married, and say to themselves, "I'm going to be at my new church four years. As the fourth year begins, my relationship with my wife will be struggling, so I'm going to find a girl in the youth group who is everything my wife is not. I will pay extra attention to this young girl and look for ways to show physical affection to her. When she figures out what's going on, then we will become involved sexually . . . safe sex, of course. I mean, this is the nineties, right? When the church finds out, I'll be fired and my wife will leave me. Oh boy, won't this be fun!"

Ever seen the bumper sticker saying, "Sex Happens"? It's sadly true. Most youth pastors don't plan their downfalls in advance. Though the "cover-up" of an ongoing affair can require a truly mind-boggling amount of planning and deception, getting into an inappropriate relationship is usually not premeditated.

Gordon MacDonald had to resign his position as president of InterVarsity Christian Fellowship when a previous inappropriate relationship became public. For him it was the epitome of a broken world experience. Being a nationally known and highly respected figure, he suffered immense shame and humiliation as the news got around. Out of his shame and struggle has come his book, *Rebuilding Your Broken World*.[4] People wondered out loud how someone who seemed to have his act together and even wrote the book, *Ordering Your Private World*, could have let his private world be so compromised and destroyed so thoroughly.

Without satisfying our morbid curiosity to know exactly what happened in his fall, MacDonald does give us some clues as to why otherwise good Christian leaders end up trading in an ounce of pleasure for a pound of pain. Part II of his book is titled "Why Worlds Break" and here are his five bottom lines.[5]

"BOTTOM LINE: Influences and moods, people and atmospheres, pressures and weariness: some or all of these, like a smoke screen, can distort what might otherwise be good thinking."

Here he notes that particularly if we travel alone away from home, the normal environment of accountability we live in is absent. Tiredness, distance from and frustration with our spouse, make us open to misbehavior.

"BOTTOM LINE: Wise people need to know how their spiritual and mental systems are apt to operate in various environments."

Mark, the youth pastor who fled the chance to give Shelley a back rub in his office, knew himself well enough to know that behind a locked office door, and with almost no chance of interruption, he would not want to limit his massage to a back rub only. He knew, too, in an instant, that she was very open to whatever might develop.

"BOTTOM LINE: When the body and emotions and the mind are stretched to the limit, the risk of sinful choices climbs out of sight."

We can handle weariness, frustration, loss, and stress up to a point, but taken together and experienced over a long time period, we may come to feel that we are entitled to some quick relief.

"BOTTOM LINE: Misbehavior may often be rooted in the undisclosed things of our past."

For example, it's easy to carry insecurity into adult life if our parents were not affirming or if we were raised in a dysfunctional family. One temporary pain reliever of deep insecurity is illicit sex.

"BOTTOM LINE: A disrespect for the power of evil is a major step toward a broken personal world."

After all, Satan is real and he delights in the destruction of Christian workers. "Your enemy the devil prowls around like a roaring lion looking for someone to devour" (1 Peter 5:8).

Sobering, isn't it? We can see how these things Gordon MacDonald talks about can work in our own lives. He points out the problem, but how do we build fences in our own lives against sexual sin? What are specific things we can do in ministry that will keep our attractions from becoming fatal ones?

Beware by being aware is first. I need to be aware that I am capable of sin, failure, and mistakes of judgment. MacDonald's "Bottom Lines" are vital cautions to us all. I try to review these bottom lines from time to time . . . mentally recalling how Satan works and what first steps down the wrong path would look like.

Second, **wonder** in our Christian lives is critically important. Recently I have been thinking about Psalm 105:5, "Remember the wonders he has done, his miracles, and the judgments he pronounced." I have been reviewing the wonders and miracles God has been doing in and around me recently. I long to see things happen in this ministry that cannot be explained by administration and organization.

If my longing is going to be fulfilled, I have to really hunger for God in my daily life. I have to be willing to take a stand and take a risk for him. I must not be lulled into a spiritual stupor by my comfortable life and predictable routine. I must never, ever, let the praise of people be a substitute for God's approval. Conversely, I must not allow critical people to become like spiritual bloodsuckers, draining the peace and presence I feel with my Lord.

One "wonder" I am thankful for today is that my teenage daughter wants to buy a T-shirt that will help her witness for Christ. Her first choice? The front of the shirt shows Jesus doing a push-up with the cross on his back. The T-shirt says, "Lord's Gym: Bench Press This!" On the back it shows a nail-pierced hand and it reads, "His Pain, Your Gain." Another girl in the youth group who has one guarantees that the shirt triggers ample witnessing opportunities!

Real accountability is third. We've already seen how real accountability can help preclude our misbehavior when it comes to handling youth group money.

If we travel alone away from home, it's important to set up accountability and reminders of the accountability we normally have at home. Phone appointments with our spouse or close friends are vital. Notes, cards, and little gifts left by us for our family and received from our family remind us of our commitments.

All Christian leaders need people or a group where honesty and vulnerability are the norm. In this context we can admit our potentially fatal attractions, seek prayer, and experience the joy that a truly clean conscience brings. The possibilities are varied for youth workers. Some will find this with other members of the church staff. Others get this from meeting regularly with youth workers. Still others will find support in a small group Bible study or fellowship group.

American Express implores us to carry one of their credit cards: "Don't leave home without it." We shouldn't leave home without a real accountability structure in place.

Last, **consistently remind yourself of the consequences of misbehavior.** Randy Alcorn, who is on the staff of Good Shepherd Community Church in Oregon, has listed the outcomes if he were to fall into sexual sin:[6]

- Grieving the Lord who redeemed me.
- Dragging his sacred name into the mud.
- One day having to look Jesus, the righteous judge, in the face and give an account of my actions.
- Following in the footsteps of these people whose immorality forfeited their ministries and caused me to shudder (list names).
- Inflicting untold hurt on Nanci, my best friend and loyal wife.
- Losing Nanci's respect and trust.
- Hurting my beloved daughters, Karina and Angie.
- Destroying my example and credibility with my children, and nullifying both present and future efforts to teach them to obey God.
- If my blindness should continue or my wife be unable to forgive, perhaps losing my wife and my children forever.
- Causing shame to my family.
- Losing self-respect.
- Creating a form of guilt awfully hard to shake. God would forgive me, but would I ever forgive myself?
- Forming memories and flashbacks that could plague future intimacy with my wife.
- Wasting years of ministry training and experience for a long time, maybe permanently.

- Forfeiting the effects of years of witnessing to my father and reinforcing his distrust for ministers that has only begun to soften by my example, but that would harden, perhaps permanently, because of my immorality.
- Undermining the faithful example and hard work of other Christians in our community.
- Bringing great pleasure to Satan, the enemy of God and all that is good.
- Heaping judgment and endless difficulty on the person with whom I committed adultery.
- Possibly bearing the physical consequences of such diseases as gonorrhea, syphilis, chlamydia, herpes, and AIDS; perhaps infecting Nanci or, in the case of AIDS, even causing her death.
- Possibly causing pregnancy, with the personal and financial implications, including a lifelong reminder of my sin.
- Bringing shame and hurt to these fellow pastors and elders (list names).
- Causing shame and hurt to these friends, especially those I've led to Christ and discipled (list names).
- Invoking shame and lifelong embarrassment upon myself.

Quite a list! If we remind ourselves from time to time about the consequences of sexual sin, we will be less likely, by God's grace, to trade an ounce of pleasure for a pound of pain.

*   *   *

In the last six chapters, I have presented a primer for youth workers who want to last. Making it in youth ministry is not only possible, it's probable as we give attention to these aspects of ministry. Successful youth ministry becomes even more likely if we have a plan.

CHAPTER ELEVEN

BLUEPRINTS FOR A FIVE-YEAR STAY

There is a delicious confusion as we arrive in a new ministry situation. There are zillions of people to greet, meet, and treat. We're moving in! We unpack our boxes . . . our sundry material possessions which, for better or worse, help make us us.

What do we do, where do we start? What should we wear our first week at the office? Should we put on our best suit and court a different board member or elder over fine French cuisine every day? Or should we instead put on our most depreciated Levi 501's and hang out at the local junior high after school? Better yet, should we don our most intelligent-looking sweater/slacks combination and forsake all that meaningless socializing? Yes, let's get down to the real task at hand and cloister ourselves in the office . . . we need time to carefully work through the Hebrew exegesis for our pending youth group study on Leviticus.

How about none of the above!

It's impossible to plan *exactly* the best approach to take at the onset of ministry, but there are some common sense items that must be on our agenda as we get started and get going in ministry.

KEEP THAT ORGAN LOFT CLEAN

One of the most important items on the list is to *never, ever* forget the James Davey Organ Loft Principle of Ministry. Never heard of it? Here it is: James Davey was my senior pastor for six years. When he was a student at Wheaton College, he was on the custodial staff of Wheaton Bible Church. It wasn't exactly a glamour job, but it did pay some of the bills. Anyway, each week he was *always* careful to clean the organ loft first and to clean it very well. The organ loft is where the money people counted the Sunday offerings. James was wise enough to know that in any church, the people who deal with the money are either at the center of influence or very close to that center. He wanted *them* to know he was doing not just a good job, but a great one.

The application to youth ministry is this: there are certain tasks, jobs, ministries, duties—call them what you will—that we *must* do as youth pastors. We may not want to, we may be more interested in something else, but if we ignore the "organ lofts" of youth ministry, soon we'll be back at the copy shop, laser printing an updated resume.

What are some of the "organ lofts" of youth ministry?

One of them is that church people have the nerve to believe that **the youth pastor will have some kind of significant ministry among church kids.** Sure, they want us to reach the world for Christ, but most of them prefer that we reach the reached before we reach the lost.

Exactly here is the smoking gun that shoots down many a ministry. One respondent to my survey wrote about the fired youth pastor at her church:

> *"Bret was running an aggressive youth outreach program. In his final year in ministry eighty-five high school kids came to Christ and were baptized. The church was not ready for this kind of growth, costs, use of building, and so on. The church was made up largely of older people who had a hard time with these other unchurched kids. This growth led to conflicts with the parents ("Why is my kid left out?"; "more Bible study needed"; "I don't want my kid around these new ones"). The parents got to the board and Bret was told he was fired. He had been there four years."*

We may feel a deep burden to reach the lost. We may want to pronounce judgment on a congregation that doesn't have our vision. We can preach, pray, threaten, lobby, and scheme—but it won't change a thing. Face it . . . most churches want us to reach the reached first. Ignore this, and we've got a dirty "organ loft."

Other "organ lofts" regarding people include not only kids, but parents and our pastors. We've already given these much greater attention in Chapters Five, Six, and Seven.

Here's another major "organ loft": Both kids and parents expect **that our ministry will have at least a hint of organization and structure.** They know they're not hiring someone with a master's degree in business administration, but they have the expectation that our ministry will demonstrate at least a faint shadow of planning ability.

Tim was in charge of both the junior and senior high youth groups. He arrived in August and in early September scheduled what was to be the premier junior high social event. So far, so good. In a youth ministry class in Bible college, he learned that when working with two youth groups the best approach is to disciple people to work in one (junior high) while you work in the other (senior high). Tim set out to follow this wise counsel. Again, so far, so good, at least in theory.

Faithful to his principles, Tim had not planned to come to this huge junior high event. But, the plans were well made (he thought) and the publicity was extensive.

It was Friday night and the appointed time of 7:00 p.m. arrived. Excited kids arrived by the carful, but no one from the staff had arrived yet. Soon fifteen minutes had passed. More kids arrived, and their parents waited, seeing that no one was in charge. Still no youth staff. Alas, at 7:30 p.m. the first youth staffer arrived and was shocked to find a bunch of leaderless kids whose patience was wearing thin. He bravely admitted that he assumed the other two staff people, a married couple, were in charge and would be on time. The parents who had waited through all this began taking their kids home at 7:45 p.m. By 8:00 p.m., all that remained was the lone staffer and two kids whose parents had dropped them off and had gone out for the evening.

At 8:05 p.m. a car drove up . . . behold . . . the staff couple arrived. They knew the event started at seven, but had gotten busy shopping and "just couldn't make it." They thought the other staffer was in charge, that they were just along to help out a little if needed.

This premier junior high event turned into a premier junior high catastrophe for Tim's ministry. He wasn't fired, but it wasn't until March that the junior high school kids and their parents had more than cynicism toward Tim. In one short hour, Tim had dug a hole that took him six months to crawl out of.

Yes, kids and parents expect a certain degree of competence from us. Ignore it, and our "organ loft" gets dirty astonishingly fast. Chapters Eight and Nine are meant to help us in the area of competence.

But all this still begs the question, doesn't it? What do we do *first?* How do we sequence and prioritize our many tasks when we come to a new ministry? Especially if this is our first ministry, we don't yet have an inborn sense of what needs to be done when. We know we don't have the luxury of working on just one item on our list for a year, ignoring all else. We can foresee that the ministry will be like a juggling act. How do we learn to be a wise juggler?

PREARRIVAL PREPARATION

Here are three important "P's" we are wise to care for *before* we change addresses to our new location.

Prayer. The kind of prayer I'm talking about is to be far more than just a traditional value like motherhood or apple pie. If we just give lip service to the idea of prayer, we need not wonder later why our ministry seems to lack spiritual impact.

Realize that the Gospel ministry is a ministry that is opposed by Satan himself. We cannot defeat him by going to seminars and reading books. No amount of intelligence or savvy on our part will give the adversary even minor inconvenience. What God does when we pray, however, is to begin to tear down the strongholds of the enemy's power and pave the way for the Holy Spirit to work. When we pray, we become armed and dangerous spiritually. We, by our praying, create no small disturbance behind enemy lines. Prayer is to be the lifeblood of our ministries. It was for Jesus, it was for Paul, and it should be for us.

We are wise to ask the church to send us a list of all the young people we'll be ministering to. Pray through this list at least three times a week. There is a double benefit here: (1) God will work as we pray, and (2) it will really speed learning their names before we arrive. For several years I have been praying for each new crop of ninth graders for weeks in advance of their welcome into senior high. The first Sunday in June comes and they arrive in senior high Sunday school. I find that when they say their first name, I know their last name already! I've already prayed for them by first and last name twenty times.

I strongly advise that we seek to find ten other youth workers or friends who will commit to pray for us daily for our first three months of ministry. We might have to reciprocate by praying for them daily too, but that's okay! It is a good feeling to know that we are not alone as we enter ministry.

Pyramid Power. Hold the phone, don't panic! I am not now advocating that we rush out to the nearest new-age bookstore and purchase some crystals to hold while we pray. No, I'm talking about a philosophy of ministry that has as its purpose to minister to young people at whatever level they are, and to move them up toward maturity in Christ.

Pyramid diagrams of youth ministry have been around a long time. I presented one to the board when I was a candidate at North Seattle Alliance Church in 1978. Currently we can find pyramid representations in books by Mike Yaconelli, Mark Senter, and SonLife Ministries.[1]

The stages or steps have different labels in different books, but what it comes down to is this:

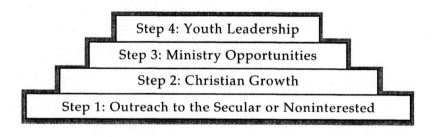

Step 4: Youth Leadership

Step 3: Ministry Opportunities

Step 2: Christian Growth

Step 1: Outreach to the Secular or Noninterested

It isn't hard to see that a ministry with all four of these stages functioning supplies significant ministry for the whole range of maturity levels in the student population.

Before arrival on the scene we should know what components of ministry already exist at our new location. We need to take what we know about our future ministry and plug the components into the pyramid as they currently function. Sunday school will likely be for Christian growth. The midweek ministry, if it exists, will probably be for growth or outreach.

With this pyramid in front of us, we can begin praying and dreaming about what needs to happen to make the ministry function well at all four stages.

Want to be radical? Make another pyramid before you arrive and title it "Parent Ministries." Let it have three steps: Step One, OUTREACH; Step Two, GROWTH; and Step Three, MINISTRY. Fill in some of your own ideas or good ones you've heard of from other ministries. For example, here is the Parent Ministry Pyramid that I am currently overseeing:

Step Three: MINISTRY

Being on the Ministry Team
Sunday School Teaching
Help for Special Events

Step Two: GROWTH

"In-House" Parent Seminars
Weekly Parent Support Group
Parent Video, Audio, and Printed Resources
Quarterly Parent Newsletter

Step One: OUTREACH
Annual Outreach Parent Seminar

Get out your calendar and pencil in a year's worth of parent ministry. Here is an example of a September to June plan:

September: Begin monthly newsletter
November: Parent Seminar: Communication Skills

January:	Parent Seminar: Panel on Rules, In-Hours, and so on
	Debut new parenting section in church library
March:	Parent Seminar: Showing Love to Teenagers
June:	Parent/Kid BBQ and Game Night

You may not have a clue as to what to say about parent/teen communication skills. That's fine . . . fake it. (Relax, just kidding!!) If you arrive in June or July, by early October you'll know someone who would be good, or you'll have access to a good parenting video.

We've talked about prayer, pyramids, and now there is one more "P" that we need to think about before arriving . . . and that is the subject of principles.

Principles. We want our ministry to meet kids where they're at and bring them up to maturity in Christ. We want to disciple them and help them grow up into him who is the Head. Great. But what does a disciple look like? How do we know one when we see one?

Get away for part of a day to a nice quiet place where you can really think and dream. Take out a sheet of paper and write down between five and ten objectives or principles that you want both yourself and the young people in your new youth group to demonstrate.

I didn't think to do this at my first church, but I made sure I did it before candidating at my second. My list of six makes no claim to being inspired . . . but since the late seventies, these objectives have guided my teaching and choices in ministry. Here is what I'm looking for.

1. That we may learn to grow in him and to walk in his kind of strength in our Christian lives. This involves a meaningful prayer life, consistent study of the Word, worship, and meaningful meditation through the day.

2. That we may know what our spiritual gifts are, as well as how to use them in our ministries in the group, in the church, and in the world.

3. That we may develop authentic Christian lifestyles characterized by a sense of balance, personal fulfillment, and yet a commitment to share in the lives of others and their needs.

4. That we may eagerly and freely share our faith with others and have a parallel concern for the lost in other lands.

5. That we be engaged in the personal discipleship of another person or group of people.

6. That we may have a satisfactory atmosphere in our families characterized by communication and openness.

These three "P's" are of more than just academic interest to me personally. The junior high pastor at our church has just resigned and there is no money to hire a replacement. So, soon I will be working with the junior highers as well as the senior highers. I am making my list of youth pastors to call to ask for daily prayer support. Pyramids are forming in my mind and soon will be on paper. I am looking at these six principles and evaluating which of them is appropriate to expect from early adolescents.

NAVIGATING YOUR FIRST MONTH

A very important request you should make is that your new church have everything planned and staffed for the *first four weeks* after your arrival. Of course, if you're starting a ministry from scratch, that won't be possible, but otherwise, go ahead and make the request. If things are covered during the first four weeks, it gives you a chance to get the feel of the programs as well as of the movers and shakers among the youths and adults.

In my first month of my first church after seminary, I succeeded in expertly alienating a huge number of people. I managed to create such a personal relations disaster that it took two years for some people to accept me. One family even left the church over my faux pas.

In this new church, I was to be in charge of the junior high, young people's (high school and college combined), and young couples groups. I had it in the back of my mind that it would be nice to eventually split off the college kids from the high schoolers. It seemed to me that twenty-four-year-olds and fifteen-year-olds were light-years apart when it came to needs. On the last day of my candidating weekend, the search committee asked what I felt their needs were. I mentioned that I thought an eventual separation of the high school/college group would be wise. They agreed, and I didn't give the matter a second thought.

My second Sunday, the Church Education Director told me there was a group of people I needed to meet with. I naively agreed and went to the meeting. Pastor Bob had gathered eight twenty-four-year-olds whom he had talked with about my plans to split the group. They were very much in favor of the split. Furthermore, they wanted it *now*.

"I was thinking maybe a big change like that would be good a year down the line, but wow, if there is this much grass roots support, let's go for it!" I responded.

Later, I made our intentions widely known. It was one of the dumbest things I've ever done.

The announcement unleashed a fire storm, a revolution, a roar of protest and disapproval. Kids yelled at me. Parents phoned me in tears. All of a sudden I was cast as the devil himself in the minds of some. Why all the stress?

You guessed it . . . the high school girls were absolutely, totally, and unalterably opposed. Yes, they gave all kinds of spiritual reasons, but the bottom line, I quickly learned, was this—high school girls hunger for college men, not for boys their own age. Upset this social configuration and all hell can break loose. So I learned that when we arrive at a new ministry there may be power blocks of people who have long been wanting a certain change. It's fine to listen, but don't promise or institute immediate change.

Of course, in the first month we will begin attending meetings with the kids and getting to know them. They need to see us enjoy ourselves with them. We can create an immense amount of goodwill by beginning a visitation program. I don't recommend we show up unannounced at the kids' homes. Another thing to avoid—don't expect them to want you to sit next to them in their school cafeteria. They don't know you well enough yet . . . the risk that you'll be an embarrassment is too great. Instead, take them out to lunch in two's or three's. Meet with them after school for ice cream or a soda. Do it in groups, as this reduces the pressure of potential silence.

Begin meeting with the pastoral staff as well, trying to understand the pressures, seasons, and stress points there.

MEETING TIME

There are two crucial meetings we are wise to have in our first four weeks.

We need to meet with the parents. They will be interested in hearing about both our testimony and about our call to ministry. They will be interested in our pyramid and principles for the kids.

They'll sit bolt upright in their seats, however, when we put our plan for ministry to parents up on the overhead. We can show our pyramid plan for them, as well as for the kids here. Handle this meeting well and some will be tempted to carry us around the church on their shoulders while others throw palm branches to cover the path ahead.

Before ending the meeting with prayer for the ministry, pass out a survey with these questions: What are some of the strengths and weaknesses of your son/daughter? What do I need to know to most effectively minister to him/her? What topics or issues would you like us to address in the parent newsletter or during the parent seminars? Do you have an area of expertise that you would be willing to share with other parents about parenting? Then, in the coming year, be sure to use their ideas and any offers of help.

It is unlikely that 100 percent of the parents will be present at this meeting. Within two days, follow up with a letter to those who were not present. Share with them everything that was discussed and show your enthusiasm for them and for parent ministries. Also, send a copy of this letter to every member of your main church board and/or elders. These meetings and letters will give you an immediate good reputation.

The other crucial meeting of the first four weeks should be **with the money people in the church.** It could be a finance committee, the church treasurer, or the financial secretary. *You* ask for the meeting. In the meeting, ask them to help you understand how the money system in the church works. Tell them you want to be absolutely scrupulous when it comes to youth group money. How and how often do they want you to report to them about finances?

In these first four weeks, we will also look again at our pyramid. We will see for ourselves how different components of the ministry are working. Most youth workers move into groups that are marginal at outreach, pretty good at growth, and poor at ministry and leadership.

Yes, it will be a busy four weeks, but profitable. We begin to get to know our people, and we begin to be known as a man or woman who keeps the "organ loft" spotless.

INTO THE FIRST YEAR

In the next eleven months of ministry, we busy ourselves working our plans. We bring high-quality, relevant Bible teaching to the young people. We do the things we need to do to communicate our love for the kids and create a healthy group environment. We work our plan for parent ministries. We learn firsthand what the needs are and we get a better feel for what the future can be. It is unrealistic to think that we will be able to start several major new components of the ministry. Our task will be to improve on the existing programs and structure. If we see the need for major change, we begin to help others to see the need and to own the proposed change as well.

In Chapter Seven, I presented my plan for working with youth leadership. If we come to a new church and find the ministry to be adult-based instead of youth-based, this shift should not be controversial. We can't really get good at pyramid Step One until the youth leadership is solid and ministry-minded.

In my first year at North Seattle Alliance Church, I instituted the discipleship training for groups of no more than seven at a time. I took them through eight weeks of intensive training. I also instituted a youth leadership plan (see Chapter Seven).

It is not uncommon for adult volunteer staff to resign when the new youth pastor comes. In my first month here, the man who was coordinating the senior high ministry took me to lunch. One by one he handed me eleven file folders and when finished he said,

"This is the happiest day of my life." Within a year he and all the others had resigned.

Like it our not, we need to give attention to recruiting adult staffers in our first year. This helps set the stage for ministry enlargement in the second. The recruitment plan I follow is a potpourri of ideas gleaned from other youth pastors. Les Christie is one of the nation's experts at it and he's even written a book entirely devoted to this subject.[2]

After assessing the needs and praying, my basic process is as follows:

The Phone or Foyer Contact. There is nothing extended about this initial contact. I simply explain that we have a real need for help in the youth ministry and I am looking to talk with people who might consider being involved. I mention when it would begin (usually at least three months from now). I ask if we could arrange a time for a personal visit so everything can be explained in detail.

The Personal Visit. I thank them for their willingness to hear more. We then discuss the specific needs the youth group has. This is no "make work" project; we really need people to get involved. I then bring out the pyramid paper along with our six objectives. People really enjoy seeing how the whole ministry fits together and what the overall purpose and plan are. This gives people the impression that the ministry is well thought out and has depth.

Then out comes the job description. We talk it through, along with the time expectations, training available, and length of tenure. I conclude with sharing some of the joys and frustrations people have who do this ministry. I ask them to think it over and pray about it.

Waiting. A week is about right.

Phone or Foyer Follow-Up. Now it is time for their answers. If they say no, I thank them for their willingness to consider. If they say yes, I'm very enthusiastic in my appreciation. We then figure out the next logical step between now and when the person is to begin.

In this first year, we can also build a parent team that will manage and plan parent ministries in year two and beyond.

In my first year here, it was the laying out of a six-year curriculum plan that turned out to be one of my best decisions. Basically, it is a two-year plan for the junior highers and a four-year plan for senior highers (see Appendix C).

YEAR TWO AND BEYOND

If we have created ownership on the part of kids and adults, they will be open to and ready for change when necessary. We look again at the weaknesses in the ministry and we design, with others, what kind of change will happen. A common year-two strategy is to begin significant outreach programs. These provide an arena in which our core kids can invite non-Christian friends. It is an arena in which marginal kids in the youth group may find enjoyment. I was so swamped in ministry with the young people when I came here that I didn't really get serious about recruiting until my second year. The scope of this aspect of the ministry is described more fully in Chapter Nine.

Year by year we can choose different aspects of the ministry to receive our intense focus. As more adults and young people share the ministry load and vision, it frees us to be creative in other areas. I used to hate Sunday school, but one year (my third) I totally revamped the whole program. It's been going well ever since.

Remember the principles or objectives we set out to accomplish? Beginning in year two and annually thereafter, it is important to actually measure how we are doing. We can get a feel for how we are doing through observation and counsel. However, the six objectives listed earlier in this chapter are actually measurable, and your list can be, too. We have developed two surveys to test how the young people at North Seattle Alliance Church are growing in each of the six areas. The first survey the kids put their names on, and they let us know issue by issue how they are doing. They tell us directly if they would like more help in a specific area. We do this survey in the fall (see Appendix D).

* * *

Our ministry pyramid and our principles serve as a guide to keep us on course as we develop the ministry God has given us. Unfortunately, many youth workers never make it through the first five years. They want to, but their ministry is cut short by the words, "You're fired." We now turn our attention to the issues of our response to the shock of firing. We will also consider how to know when we should take the initiative and resign. Finally, we will look at how the renewed youth worker can learn to stay.

PART THREE

KNOWING WHEN TO LEAVE; LEARNING HOW TO STAY

CHAPTER TWELVE

WHAT TO DO IF
THE AX FALLS ON YOU

"I had been at the church as youth pastor for several years and really felt that God's blessing was on the ministry. The youth group had grown and the kids knew I loved them and it appeared to me that they loved me, too.

"Our senior pastor served our church for over twenty years and finally retired. I was sorry to see him go but the board emphasized that they wanted me to stay. They didn't expect that all other staff members would resign when a change came at the top. That made me feel secure because I know other guys who have to pack their bags if their pastor resigns.

"The church as a whole and the youth group actually continued to grow during the interim and it continued to grow when our new pastor came.

"I liked the new pastor a lot. He was about the same age as I, which was a little strange, but I thought we would become great friends.

"I don't remember exactly the day I figured out I was in trouble, but it blew me away when I heard some people in the church talking to the pastor about me and the 'problems' in the youth group. I approached him on the subject. The big problem these people were having with me and the youth group was that we played 'Christian rock' during youth events. True, we did. But, yikes, it wasn't Christian heavy metal . . . no Stryper and Bloodgood was ever played on the youth group compact disc player. Even Petra was rarely on. We listened to Michael W. Smith, Amy Grant, and even some good old Sandi Patti. Not exactly music to slam dance and headbang to, right?

"Well, these people found others in the church who thought all contemporary Christian rock music was straight from hell. They obtained cassette tapes from speakers who agreed with their point of view and began to circulate them. Soon, more and more people became alarmed.

"What bothered me is that they didn't bring their concerns to me. We could never discuss this in an open forum. They took their concerns to the pastor. He never brought it to the elders or the board. He rarely spoke with me about it.

"At some point in his mind, he must have decided that to preserve the unity of the church I had to go. He put this on the agenda of a board meeting. I guess this 'anti-Christian youth music' group had been lobbying board members, too. Several had heard the tapes that were circulating. Anyway, they agreed with him that we needed to keep unity, and so I had to go.

"The board met on a Thursday night. The pastor told me Friday morning I was fired. Friday evening began a long-planned youth retreat that I had to go on and lead. I could barely bring myself to get on the church bus, but somehow I managed.

"That night, at the retreat, I told the kids. Many of them cried, the volunteer staff was blown away, and kids were angry, too. They wanted to stage a coup and it was all I could do to keep our focus on the Lord during the retreat.

"Needless to say, it was a crisis for me and my family."

NORMAL FEELINGS

Crisis is an understatement! Paul, whose story is above, found this to be one of the biggest problems he'd faced as a Christian. His ministry was blessed by God, being affirmed by people, too. How could a group of people, people who didn't even have teenagers in the youth group, manipulate to get him fired? He understood how it happened, but how could something so clearly unjust and unfair take place in the church—his church?

Paul's situation is not uncommon. Many firings are the result of a noisy minority. This noisy minority knows how church politics work. They know how to play ecclesiastical hardball and with whom. They make their moves, form their alliances, map their game plans, and pretty soon we're out.

In other cases, it's we who are the problem. We make a series of big mistakes, we demonstrate expertise in incompetence, and we get fired as a result.

No matter what the reason, we will experience a cycle of feelings in the aftermath. *Psychology Today* says getting fired is like experiencing a death in our immediate family.[1] I have personally known many who have lost their jobs in youth ministry. They cycle through Elisabeth Kubler-Ross's stages of grief.[2] It really is like a death and the feelings follow a predictable sequence:

Denial. "This can't be true, there must be a mistake. Surely they'll come to their senses, or someone will come to my defense. This stuff happens to others, but it can't happen to me."

Anger. "This isn't fair. I want to go to the congregation and scream about how I've been mistreated. I want revenge. I want to see these people grovel. I feel like saying, with the psalmist, '. . . happy is he who repays you for what you have done . . . he who seizes your infants and dashes them against the rocks' (Psalm 137:8-9). My being fired can't be God's will! How can a good God who's supposed to be in control allow this to happen?"

Bargaining. "Okay, God—yes, I've made mistakes. If I promise to improve, could you please somehow get my job back? I'll do anything for you . . . I'll be more zealous in evangelism. I'll try harder to please the parents. I'll do anything you want, even tithe 20 percent. Just don't let me face the embarrassment of this. When word of this gets out to other youth pastors. . . ."

Depression. "They fired me. I'm not good enough to serve God in a church. Yes, it was unfair, but if I were really doing a good enough job it couldn't have happened. Maybe I've misread 'God's will' all along. Maybe I was kidding myself about trying to be a youth pastor. Maybe I'm not good enough to do anything for God."

Acceptance. "Well, I guess I need to get on with my life. What can I learn from this mess?"

How intense will our feelings be if we get fired? Researchers who keep their jobs by studying those who lose theirs have come up with several predictors.[3]

Getting the ax won't be so painful if:
- It really isn't our fault. (For example, the church runs out of money.)
- We can see it coming. (For example, if the pastor resigns, and all staff must go, too.)
- We've got a successful track record and we don't feel that getting another position will be a major problem.
- There are a lot of negatives about our current position, and being free from the hassles will be a relief.

Of course, the flip sides of all these are true, too. If we love our job, didn't see it coming, and got fired for unjust cause—we are in for a major internal struggle.

Let's look at two kinds of firings and what an appropriate response for each can be.

MY MISTAKE

I have experienced enough mishaps and disasters in ministry to fill a series of thick books. I've never been fired, but there sure have been people who would have smiled to hear the news of my "feeling called" to exit.

When I was twenty, I was a part-time junior high youth group director in a church while I was attending the University of Washington. My friend Steve and I had a nice apartment. The senior high director, Tami, and I had become *very* close friends. She was having some financial problems, so Steve and I invited Tami to come live with us until she had enough money to get a place of her own. She slept on our living room sofa, nothing immoral was going on, and I didn't give it a second thought . . . until one Sunday morning Tami and I were asked to meet with a subcommittee of the elders. Funny thing, they had not called the meeting to tell us what a wonderful job we were doing as youth directors.

When I was thirty, it was my pleasure to take the twelfth graders on a Grad Overnight to a posh resort in British Columbia, Canada. A large group had signed up, and we were having a great time. That night I didn't give them any rules, in-hours, or expectations for behavior. I went to bed around midnight congratulating myself for being such a with-it youth pastor. About 2:00 a.m., my wife, who was also along, said she thought we had some people missing. I grudgingly put on my clothes, and a head count showed that three kids were gone. I eventually found Scott a mile down the strip, dancing in a nightclub with a girl he'd picked up. I never did find Linda and her boyfriend Jason. They sauntered in about 5:30 a.m., very tired. When Linda and Jason got off the bus back at church she thanked me for the *especially* good time they had! You can imagine what was thought and said by parents as this news got out.

When I was thirty-nine, we had a "multiple choice" social in which kids chose their activity. We dropped one group off at the roller rink. They knew when I would pick them up, but that was all. I didn't have an adult scheduled to be with them. After all, what can go wrong at a roller rink? It didn't occur to me to let them know how to reach me in case of a problem. Well, there was nearly gang warfare at the rink that night. Our girls were being harassed and one, Barb, was slammed to the floor. Unfortunately, her arm was broken. Her parents were out to dinner, and the rink wouldn't call for aid without parental permission. So there Barb sat for two hours surrounded by others in our group as gang members hurled insults and racial taunts. My lack of planning and false assumptions spelled disaster for that one. Fortunately, her parents were forgiving.

No, I have not been fired, but I have made mistakes. When we make mistakes, especially major mistakes, there are four crucial responses we must make. We must make these responses whether or not our error results in job termination.

1. Repentance and Restoration. "Therefore, if you are offering your gift at the altar and there remember that your brother has something against you, leave your gift there in front of the altar. First go and be reconciled to your brother; then come and offer your gift" (Matthew 5:23-24).

A major mistake means people are rightfully offended. In my three examples above, I had to acknowledge my error and seek forgiveness. Sure, Linda and Jason knew better than to use the Grad Overnight as an opportunity to explore their sexuality, but I was the one who didn't give them any in-hours, didn't tell them *not* to be in each other's room, and didn't outline general Christian behavior expectations.

When we err, even if "it's not all our fault," we must humbly acknowledge our error and seek the forgiveness of those whom we have offended. A piece of wisdom from Gordon MacDonald: "The freest person in the world is one with an open heart, a broken spirit, and a new direction in life."[4] Getting the slate wiped clean before God and people is basic to recovery.

2. The Right Question. The right question to ask when we make a major-league mistake is this: What can I learn from this mess? We might be able to do this only after we've cycled through Ross's stages of grief to the end, but we must eventually ask it.

I've learned a great deal this way over the years: churches prefer that their youth directors not live in sin; kids need to hear the guidelines in retreat settings; and when I split the group on an event, each group should have a staffer and they need to know emergency procedures.

3. Career Reflection. If we have made a mistake serious enough to warrant job termination, it behooves us to consider our own future plans. Is the ministry really for us?

Sam loved kids, but he hated organization and paperwork. The church fired him for incompetence. Sam reflected on his life. He wasn't organized, and honestly, he didn't want to ever be that organized. He got a good construction job as a laborer and is very content. He helps at a different church as a volunteer and is very happy with his life.

We may have entered into ministry without a clear picture of what was ahead. Getting fired sure helps us see what people expect of their youth pastors. Now that we're smarter by our experience, do we really feel full-time youth work is still our calling?

4. How Can I Make Sure This Doesn't Happen Again? In terms of supervision on the job, youth pastors are more like managers than assembly-line workers. A manager has a boss, but not one who checks on progress several times a day. The assembly-line worker, on the other hand, is checked throughout the workday. The freedom we enjoy as youth workers is both a blessing and a curse.

It's a curse because some of us may need more direct supervision than others, and we easily wander off course if we don't have it.

"How can I make sure this doesn't happen again?" By setting up an accountability structure in our next ministry. We might need to meet twice weekly with the senior pastor. A weekly or monthly gathering for support and accountability with other youth workers may suffice. Whatever—we must admit our need for more structure if that is the case.

In addition to accountability, we need regular performance feedback from our church. Now hold the phone—don't panic. I'm not talking about informal and subjective criticism. God only knows how many families have roast pastor for dinner every Sunday after church and how little good comes from these conversations.

What I am talking about is a regularly scheduled time when we get some objective feedback about how we are seen by others in our ministry. Many churches do it annually. Some churches do it twice a year for new staff.

The church I serve has an annual performance appraisal and it takes place in four steps.

1. A survey is sent to about thirty people who have regular contact with me in the church (see Appendix E). These people are the ones on the volunteer youth staff, key parents, key kids, and ministry staff. Objective multiple-choice questions make up the majority of the questionnaire, but there is also opportunity for people to comment at any length they choose about strengths or weaknesses they observe.

2. Returned surveys (usually about 50 percent) are compiled by our pastor's secretary, and the senior pastor reviews them with me.

3. Together we agree on action steps to shore up weak areas. I am held accountable for carrying out those action steps.

4. The results of the survey and my interview with the pastor are conveyed to the Personnel and Policy Committee of our board.

Two years ago several comments about me that were a cause for concern came back on the surveys. On the statement, "He is too busy to talk with me," several people checked "always" or "often." Other written comments expanded on that theme.

The action step my pastor and I agreed on was agonizing for me. After services, instead of dashing through the narthex on to my next project or meeting, I was to just stand around for a while and talk. I did this to the best of my ability and sure enough, on the most recent appraisal, not one person gave me negative feedback about being too busy.

The performance appraisal flagged a blind spot I had in ministry and gave me an opportunity to correct it before it became a major issue. This questionnaire is used in many churches around the country.[5]

NOT MY MISTAKE

Paul's response to the unjust firing described at the beginning of this chapter was gracious and mature. He chose not to trigger a letter-writing campaign against the pastor. He discouraged the youths and sponsors from staging a lynching of the board. He was determined to affirm three truths in this crisis: (1) Life isn't always fair, even in the church; (2) God can use injustice done to me as a guide for future direction; and (3) Vengeance is not mine, but God's—those that instigated my firing are accountable to God, not me.

It would be hard to imagine a more reasonable response. It resulted in a great amount of peace in Paul's life. It released to God all the unfairness, injustice, and cruelty he experienced. "What a spineless response!" you may say. Well, maybe. Yes, if Martin Luther had chosen to remain passive, the Reformation might not have happened. Sure, where would we be without courageous people in our history like Martin Luther King, Jr.? I don't know exactly when it's better to fight than switch. But I do know that God doesn't call very many people to be prophets.

Paul did some others things right as he went through being fired. First, he told his children right away. Five- and seven-year-olds don't understand church politics, but they do see a difference in a dad or mom who is laboring under a crushing load. Outplacement counselors encourage their clients to tell children right away, since they'll notice something is wrong anyway.[6]

Paul broke the news to his kids the day after he got back from the retreat. "Some people in the church felt that your dad was not a good youth pastor. The kids and the parents did, but these people made the church ask me to leave. Most people in the church like me, and I know it doesn't seem fair that I have to leave. But we know as a family, God will take care of us, and the church is paying me for several months so we won't have to worry about money."

Second, he decided to take some time off. The church gave him a generous severance settlement, so he didn't have to look for a job immediately. Being fired unjustly is a stressful, soul-wrenching experience. The mind and body need time to recover. Paul took some extra time to be with his wife and family. They took some weekend trips. They got reacquainted as a family.

Third, he decided not to hold the injustice of this church against all other churches. Loving ministry and still feeling called by God, he decided to seek another ministry opportunity. He reasoned that there would be plenty of unfairness in secular jobs too, so why leave what he truly loved to do?

I know of some who have been so shattered by an unjust firing they cannot even consider returning to church ministry. About 30 percent of those who are fired decide not to seek employment in church ministry again. Travis told me of his story and his decision to seek a secular job. "My shoulders just aren't big enough to carry the knowledge that this stuff goes on in the church."

EXITING WITH STYLE

Do we want another ministry position? Seventy percent of those who get fired do. Though we might be tempted to exit with a scathing rebuke to the church and the pastor, we'd better resist, if we want to be in church ministry again. Going out in a blaze of glory is fine if we're called to be a prophet and anxious to burn our bridges behind us. The blaze of glory approach might be fun, spectacular, deeply satisfying, and even righteous, but it won't get us a job later on in another church.

If we want a future ministry, the best defense is a good offense. We should ask the church to write a letter of recommendation for us. It should outline our strengths and ministry successes. It should honestly give the reason we were fired. If we were fired for our own mistake, this is one of the first things we would discuss with a prospective new church. "I made a big mistake at Valley Presbyterian, but God has taught me a great deal in the process. I'm a better person for it. Here is what happened, and here is what I am doing to make sure that it never happens again."

If we are applying to a church in a denomination that has a placement procedure, the proper person should receive two letters: the recommendation letter from the previous church, plus a cover letter from us explaining what we have learned and how we will be better for the experience.

Covering up our past may work for a while. Eventually, however, someone in our new church will learn the truth and our cover-up will damage credibility.

* * *

We've talked at length about the response to being fired. If we're fired, we have no choice but to leave. If we're not fired, though, how do we know if we should move on? What are the signs, both internal and external, that may point the way out the door?

CHAPTER THIRTEEN

READING THE SIGNS: WHEN IS IT TIME TO LEAVE?

"Len, I don't know when I've ever been so discouraged." Liz sat slumped down in her chair as if the weight of the world was literally upon her shoulders.

"I'm usually happy, up, and things don't get me down for long. This is different."

We were at a youth pastor's meeting. I knew something was wrong the minute she walked in the door. During the meeting she had smiled and laughed when it was appropriate, but it wasn't hard to tell a war was going on inside her. It was like someone had pulled the plug and her usual sparkle was draining away.

I'm no counselor, yet I tried to give her some perspective. She had been at her church six months . . . and was right on schedule in terms of the morale curve trough (Chapter Two). Furthermore, it was November and here in soggy Seattle, Seasonal Affective Disorder claims many victims. It's a cruel month, and I tried to help her see that she and the people in her church were filtering everything through a negative grid.

"I know it hurts, Liz, but try to hang in there. I really think things will improve as you get into the new year."

She thanked me for my advice. Her face and posture brightened.

I saw Liz again three months later in February. Being late, I didn't get a chance to speak with her before the meeting, but I could tell she was feeling a lot better. She sparkled again, was genuinely involved in the meeting, and seemed fully alive.

"Len," I said to myself, "you're sure smart. Gosh, look how you helped Liz. Everything is fine with her now and she had almost bailed out." During all these internal congratulations I felt tempted to remind God how lucky he was to have someone so insightful on his side. "Yesssirreee, I'm sooo goooood."

When Liz's turn came at prayer request time, I was certain she would share the wonderful victory she was having over her former negative feelings. What she said instead jolted me.

"The reason I'm so happy today is that I resigned last week. I gave them two month's notice, but for all practical purposes, I'm outta there!"

Oops.

Afterward she came up to me to fill in the rest of the story.

"My new pastor has turned out to be one of the most controlling people I've ever met. He likes to dominate. He needs to win in every situation. He watches over my every move. He is so darn insecure it makes me sick. I feel like there is a big dark cloud in the room if he is there. His wife is the church secretary. She tries to order me around, too. I feel like I'm going to suffocate."

Assuming things were at least half as bad as she said, her decision to quit was probably a good one. To stay would have created an immense amount of internal struggle for her. This is not to say it is wrong to have internal struggle, but her situation looked hopeless. A sixty-year-old insecure and autocratic senior pastor is not likely to become warm, loving, and democratic anytime soon. Liz still believed in miracles, but to believe that her pastor would change required a leap of faith further than even she could make. At thirty-one, Liz had had enough life experience to know when it was worth the effort to try to change a situation. She felt she was smart enough to know when to go as well.

Leavings. They happen all the time. How do we know if it is time for us to move on? Let's start with the negative first.

DON'T LEAVE BECAUSE OF THESE THINGS

The affable Duffy Robbins, a youth ministry expert if there ever was one, suggests we should stay, not go, when one of these four things happen.[1]

Attendance Plateau or Decline. I had the silly idea that while my first church would be more of a learning experience, I could expect nonstop numerical youth ministry growth in my second church. That bubble popped in my fourth year. In one sense, I guessed right about attendance: it would be highest in the fall, down a bit in winter, down more in spring, and down a lot in summer. What I assumed, however, was that with each new school year, the attendance curve would be higher than the previous year. If it was, all was well. My fourth year stats were below my third year stats and I began to get nervous.

What I eventually learned is this: at least in this church and in my ministry, youth ministry attendance reflects pretty accurately what is happening with Sunday morning worship attendance. If the church is growing, my stats for Sunday school, midweek, and socials grow. If the church is plateaued, my stats plateau. If the church is down, so is the youth ministry. As I write this, attendance is down substantially (40 percent) from three years ago in our church. Youth group attendance is down too, by about 20 to 25 percent. I've learned not to take this personally. What goes down, will come up!

Someone Makes You Miserable. It is very hard—very very hard—to handle our first experience of someone making us miserable. We must understand that it is just part of ministry. It happens to senior pastors, it happens to youth pastors. We manage to cross someone and he or she purposefully tries to undermine and discourage us. It may be outright war, or it may be subtle, covert operations, but this person is against us nonetheless. If we never experience this in ministry, we are the exception, not the rule.

I got my first battlefield experience in week number two at my first church. Remember the switch to a separate college group described in Chapter Eleven? It wasn't one person who wanted me out, it was a whole lynch mob.

Without doubt, the greatest issue that has galvanized people against me is that of contemporary Christian music. Perhaps you're in a ministry situation where everyone loves music with energy. If so, count your blessings. I'm in a ministry where a small minority believes that music with energy is by definition satanic. The vast majority of people in our church are very supportive of the music and of our ministry. The frustrated few, however, have definitely made themselves known to me over the years.

Another Church Offers a Higher Salary. If we stay around in youth ministry and do a good job, we can be sure other churches will want our services. If we honestly can not feed, clothe, and house our family on our salary, a move to a better paying church makes sense. If our needs are being met, however, the offer of more money should not automatically be equated with God's call.

If a church calls and offers us a blank check we should be ready to tell them we are not for sale.

When We're Hurt. If I moved every time I felt pain in ministry, I would be living in an RV. Then I could just unplug the hookup, go to the post office with a change of address, and be on the road again. Pain, like criticism, is part of ministry. In fact, ministry is one of the occupations best able to break our hearts again and again and again.

It hurts when leadership youths decide to try on the lifestyle of drugs and alcohol. It's painful to walk through the corridors of the psych ward looking for a fifteen-year-old who's attempted suicide. It's agonizing to hold a sobbing mother as her brain-dead son lies motionless before her, a machine pumping air into him and sucking it out again.

It's no fun to cry because you dearly miss those who've just graduated out of the group. It's mind numbing when you hear that sweet sister Sue is organizing a phone campaign against you among the parents. It's no party when people say things are fine to your face and then slander you when you're not around. It's awfully hard to see good people, whom you love and need, move away or leave the church in anger. All this is just a tiny slice of what has been my ministry portion over the years.

Pain serves many positive purposes in our Christian lives. God whispers to us in our pleasure, but yells to us in our pain. There is an experience of God that only seems to come when our hearts are broken. Bad things can produce good in us if we cooperate with our loving Father and let him take us in our brokenness and make us a little more like him.

So, those are situations that should *not* cause us to resign. Now let's turn to things that should.

IT'S OKAY TO LEAVE
BECAUSE OF THESE THINGS

Experience one or more of these things and it may be time to move on.

It's certainly possible to **outgrow youth ministry.** Tony Campolo says it best: "Many youth workers enter the ministry to satisfy emotional needs that result from immaturity. As they outgrow these immature emotional needs that have been gratified in youth ministry, they find that youth work loses its capacity to excite them."[2] What are some immature emotional needs we may eventually outgrow?

The need to be the recipient of opposite sex adoration is one underlying reason some get into youth ministry. We may have been nothing but a nerd in high school and hardly ever dreamed of "making it" with the opposite sex. Things change, though, when we're twenty-two, have a hot car, and a nice apartment. Fifteen- and sixteen-year-olds now think we're cool, desirable, and they love to be with us. Campolo continues, "I recall feeling a certain dizzy exhilaration from having high school girls 'turn on' to me as I exercised what I egotistically considered to be charismatic leadership. . . . A decade later, the thrill associated with generating erotic reactions from teenagers had dissipated, and one of the emotional payoffs of youth ministry was gone for me forever."[3]

Similarly, we may outgrow the thrill of youth activities. If we were not part of the socializing crowd in high school, it is easy to feel we missed out on all the fun when growing up. Youth ministry gives us a second chance at this fun. Although not exactly a valid reason for entering ministry, it is one of the emotional payoffs many feel. It's a high, though, that doesn't last very long.

Some enter ministry with a need to control and show dominance. Youth ministry is certainly a place to do it. As we grow in Christ, however, and our hearts mature, we may feel less of a need to enjoy watching other people follow our orders.

There are other situations that make it proper for us to leave.[4] A **violation of our integrity** is one of these. We may come to the church believing that the Sunday morning service needs to be solely for Christian nurture. Our pastor might come back from a conference and switch to preaching primarily to non-Christians. This is a prime example of a difference in philosophy of ministry. If the issue is important enough to us, we'd better move on. It is important to be able to support the senior pastor, and if we can't, someone has got to go. In my friend Liz's situation, her relationship with her senior pastor became an issue of integrity and she had to move on.

Another example . . . I could never minister in a church that had a policy against contemporary Christian music. For me, it is a crucial tool of youth ministry and it would be impossible to serve in a church that didn't support this conviction.

The needs of our family should play a big part in our decision to stay or go. I really loved my first church. It was in Vancouver, British Columbia. I loved the church, the people, and the city. Yes, I was eventually accepted and loved by the people who wanted to lynch me and the farewell service was a tearjerker. One of my main reasons for leaving was that I could not figure out how I could be a good father and carry the kind of schedule I had there.

I learned that evenings at home were very important to my wife. Being in charge of junior high, senior high, college, and couples left me free only one or sometimes two nights a week. My marriage could subsist on this basis, but there is no way I could see being a father with that schedule. When I was a candidate at my second church, my first question to the board was, "How important is it to you that I have a family life?" They answered generically. I later pressed the point: "How many nights a week do you expect your pastors to be home with their families?" When they answered, "At least three," I almost said, "Where do I sign?!"

If our relationship with the young people no longer exists, we should move on. Some of us seem capable of relating to young people well no matter how old we get. Others find the leap just too large and so personal relationships suffer. Kids will sense our reluctance like a horse senses fear in an inexperienced rider. If we can't make and maintain good relationships with kids, we should probably look for another sort of ministry or another field of work.

Of course, **God's will** ought to figure into our thinking in some way. Unfortunately, God usually doesn't FAX his specific will to us. We are left to try to figure things out ourselves. We take the feelings of our heart; we share our soul with our spouse and other close friends; we read Scripture looking for a verse; and we try by these ways to determine God's will. For some, it's a clear-cut process and the leading seems unmistakable. For others, doubt and uncertainty remain and we make our decisions with much hesitancy. Either way, God can bless.

I am not a "dot theory" believer when it comes to God's will. I believe that if we are growing in him, the desires of our heart will reflect the heart of God. He can use us in Denver as well as in Chicago. His will for us, rather than being a specific place at a specific time, is better described as a range of options. He wants us to be in ministry and it is our job to find the place that will maximize our gifts and abilities.[5]

I do know that feelings are not a guarantee of God's will. When I got the first phone call from my second church, I just had a feeling it would work out well. It did and I've been here thirteen years. A couple of years ago, though, I gave my resume to another church that was on the hunt for a youth pastor. I was absolutely sure it was going to work out well. I had a good feeling about it, and so did my wife. Mentally I began to pack my bags. Well, I was one of fifty applicants. Five months later, I was one of the final six. My heart sank when the letter came informing me I was not one of the final two.

The senior pastor's resignation may properly trigger our resignation as well. Some churches expect staff members to submit their resignations when the head pastor does. The new pastor has the option, then, of keeping the team or bringing in his or her own people. It's always good to understand the process before we come to a new church. My second question to the board at North Seattle Alliance Church was, "What happens to me when the top man leaves?" They said that they'd find a new pastor to fit the existing staff. I was sure glad I asked . . . my senior pastor read his resignation letter three weeks after my arrival.

Loss of vision should also make us consider leaving. Many things help us have vision. Included are enough sleep; taking our day off; enjoying good vacations; a good family life; and good relationships with the kids, the pastor, and the parents of our ministry. A good devotional life and quality friendships are important to vision as well. If we are doing all of these and the vision still dims, it may be time to pray about either a renewed vision or a different location for a new vision.

Now that we've considered all of these aspects, let's follow the heart of one youth pastor who originally thought he was a "lifer," but later changed his mind.

ONE MAN'S STORY

David Olshine was the youth pastor of a church in Ohio.[6] He confesses, "I was one of those lifers. I loved youth work. I read all the journals; led scores of retreats; spoke at youth group meetings, clubs, and rallies; served as chaplain for a high school football team; did youth evangelism; led small and large youth groups; and even wrote a book for youth. My friends figured I'd be in youth work forever. Not surprisingly, then, when I began to confide to my lifer friends that I was considering leaving youth ministry, they laid on the guilt. . . ."

On the way home from a trip to the Holy Land, Olshine realized his interests were changing. He pictured himself showing his slides to a bunch of rowdy and disrespectful junior high school kids back home. It was not a happy thought. When he honestly looked at his life and ministry, the need for a change became clear.

He was restless and impatient. Putting up with youth culture and the way kids behave had become more difficult. He was tired of not seeing much fruit in this labor of frustration. Loss of vision went right along with this increasing restlessness. His ministry was going great, but it just did not excite him any more. Youth ministry resources that used to interest him no longer kindled a desire to take the ministry further.

Olshine admitted to being bored. He wasn't burned out. He had regular days off, adequate family time, and a large volunteer staff. "Teenagers became dull to me," he said. A cousin to his boredom was his feeling of lack of challenge. He wanted to dig into the Bible and preach it. His youth group wanted a steady diet of love, sex, and dating.

Finally, he admitted that perhaps his nine years in youth ministry had been a season in his life. It had been a good season and much was accomplished. Yet seasons change, people change, and he found growing in him the desire to minister to every age within a church, not just teenagers. He couldn't picture himself as a forty-two-year-old youth pastor with his own daughter in the high school group. Olshine is now the senior pastor of a Methodist church in Ohio.

* * *

The last question we turn to now is this—how do we stay fresh, handle the pressures, and keep the drive alive during our first years of ministry? How do we make our youth ministry *really* successful and rewarding? In the last chapter, we will see how we can set a personal renewal trajectory that will guide our course through all our years in ministry.

CHAPTER FOURTEEN

THE RENEWED YOUTH WORKER

I chose to enter the sanctuary about a minute late. Our elder board had called for an evening of prayer and I was pleased to see so many show up. We all knew why we were there . . . to pray in small groups for healing in our nearly split church body. We would be in small groups according to the row we were sitting in.

As my eyes scanned the crowd, my insides had a pre–stomach-flu heaviness. My heart was beating so fast I could feel it throbbing in my chest. There he was. The man who just two weeks before had posted an open letter to the congregation that condemned the youth ministry. Painful instant replays of the last two weeks whirled in my head. Just a few days earlier, the chairman of the elders informed me they had received the results of a phone campaign organized by this man. The callers wanted me out.

"Lord," I prayed as I began to move, "thank you that I don't have to follow Satan's strategy for destroying my relationship with you and this church." I walked slowly toward the front, came to his row, and slid over to sit right next to him. He and his wife looked at me in disbelief.

Was my action the epitome of stupidity? Was it a calculated political maneuver designed to impress people in the pews? Well, I know it wasn't the latter and I pray it wasn't the former. It was, instead, a sincere attempt to act on a belief that God could work. I believed he could work a miracle in what otherwise looked like an impossibly fractured relationship.

If we are going to successfully survive our first five or ten or fifteen years in youth ministry, we must learn the secrets of renewal. A renewed heart and spirit make it possible for us to not be blown away by criticism. A renewed heart keeps us going when we are starved to see results and go hungry instead. A renewed heart makes it possible to keep perspective when it seems like our world is falling apart.

Renewal comes to us in our first or fifteenth year of ministry as we give priority to these practical essentials.

Marriage and Time. Nearly 80 percent of the fired youth pastors I surveyed were married. The allotment of our time plays a huge role in our personal well-being, whether we are single or married.

> My husband is a full-time youth director. He is extremely dedicated and spends between fifty and seventy hours a week with young people.
>
> I think the reason he is so successful with kids is that he is always available to them, always ready to help when they need him.
>
> That may be why attendance has more than doubled in the past year. He really knows how to talk their language. This past year he would be out two and three nights a week talking with kids until midnight. He's always taking them to camps and ski trips and overnight camp outs. If he isn't with kids, he's thinking about them and preparing for his next encounter with them.
>
> And if he has any time left after that, he is speaking or attending a conference where he shares with others what God is doing through him. When it comes to youth work, my husband has always been 100 percent.
>
> I guess that's why I left him.
>
> There isn't much left after 100 percent.
>
> Frankly, I just couldn't compete with God.[1]

There is no small amount of stress and tension in the marriages of youth workers. Much of the stress relates to time and its use . . . or misuse. Time is an issue for the single youth worker as well: a consistent misallocation puts us on the fast track to burnout.

Over my years of ministry, marriage, and then parenthood, I have learned my own time limitations and capabilities. For me, the comfort zone is in the fifty to fifty-five hours-per-week range. This is about the same as the other pastors on our staff, and normal for people in our congregation who are mid- or upper-level executives.

Stress between my wife and me over the use of time took a major nosedive when I instituted the "square system" of time use.

A week (Monday through Saturday) has eighteen squares: three squares a day, one for morning, afternoon, and evening.

	MON	TUES	WED	THURS	FRI	SAT
AM				/		
AFT				/		/
PM	/			/	/	

Since I know what meetings I have to attend on a regular basis, and we plan the youth calendar three to six months in advance, it is possible to mark out my off-time several months in advance. In the example above, you see a normal week for me, minus Sunday. It is a standard "six-square week." There are six blocks of time that I am off. I know myself well enough to know that feelings of unrest and frustration will begin to grow if I have less time off than this. Occasionally, I'm also off Tuesday night and Saturday night.

Once these squares are filled on my own church calendar, I take it home and enter this information on our family calendar. This represents my commitment to my wife and family. If someone phones my wife and wants us to get together, she knows when I am involved at church and when I am free by simply looking at the calendar.

Except for emergencies (like death or a family crisis situation) that require immediate intervention, I almost never change the schedule once it is entered on the family calendar. If someone wants to see me or have a meeting on a night that is already marked off, I simply say, "I have another commitment on that night." My commitment may be to go shopping with my wife, play

"Uno" with my daughters, or clean the garage, but I treat these commitments as seriously as any others.

This commonly means I double or even triple schedule things on the nights that I do work. Wednesdays are usually like that. After youth group there may be an Adult Christian Education meeting (also my responsibility) at 8:45 p.m. When that gets done at 9:45 p.m., I may go out for salad with one of the interns who wants some one-on-one time. Saturday morning is usually triple scheduled: breakfast with a kid, a youth leadership meeting, and then a counseling appointment.

If there is a retreat or overnighter in one week, I take a "comp" day the next week. It is an extra day off for recovery and family time.

At my first church, I was usually out six nights a week. This was hard on both my wife and me. The senior pastor assured me I could come in late in the morning instead of at 8:30 a.m., but I found that mornings just didn't make up for evenings.

Your tastes and needs for time use are no doubt different than mine, but the point is this—*we need to figure out what we need*. If we are married, our spouses should enter into this figuring as well.

Personal renewal only happens if we continually have the sense that our work time and off time have rhythm and balance.

Leave Your Work at the Office. Archibald Hart in his book, *Adrenaline and Stress*,[2] explains how important it is for the human body to have times when adrenaline is not being dumped into the bloodstream. In a typical day of ministry, our adrenal glands work hard most of the time. When we come home we need to let our adrenaline come down. To do this it is important to have our home be our home, whether it is a studio apartment or a five-bedroom rambler.

One problem about home, though, is the phone. In my first year of ministry, I succeeded in creating a great amount of stress for my wife by coming home from the office with a list of ten phone calls to make.

"But dear," I'd say, "these people are at school or work all day and supper time or evening is when they are free. I've got no choice but to call them now. I'm a pastor, and that's the way it is."

Funny thing—my reasonable explanations didn't reduce the tension in our marriage over this issue. What reduced the tension was this—I stopped making calls at home! Sure, occasionally I still do, but it's very rare. How did I manage to do it? I began making phone calls at church before or after meetings. Saturday morning is also an excellent time for calling kids and adults. (Caution: Don't call adults before 9:00 a.m. and kids before 10:30 a.m.)

Do Something that Will Stretch Your Faith. It is easy to get complacent in ministry after the first two or three years. We get into a pattern, see some success, set the cruise control on "coast," and relax. Unfortunately this is a plan that more easily produces rust than growth.

In the first two or three years of a new ministry, nearly everything is truly new, and we know we need to be on our knees in prayer. We should never be too good or too experienced to believe we need to humbly come to God in prayer for the ministry.

Every year I try to do something in ministry that forces me to get on my knees and pray. It needs to be something I've never done before, something that has no guarantee of success, and something that reminds me of my total dependence on God.

Many youth workers easily gravitate toward campus involvement to make contact with kids. I avoided that until the year I decided to be a library volunteer. The night before my first day at school my nightmare was vivid: I saw myself walking down the hall . . . there were youth group members ahead . . . they saw me and quickly turned the other way to avoid being seen with me. Whew! I was so glad when my alarm went off!

Enjoy the Troops. Laughter and fun are vital parts of a healthy life. Youth workers who honestly enjoy their young people find themselves energized by time with them.

It is easy to get overwhelmed by the problems of young people. There are those who cause problems and suck us dry of energy and optimism. This is toxic to renewal and we must guard against letting the negative overwhelm us.

I love to have fun. I enjoy long hours of laughter, "Trivial Pursuit," and storytelling on the church bus. I've been known to start a water fight in a posh hotel at 2:00 a.m. I've brought a squirt gun to Bible study. I love to take kids to places they've never been and just watch them enjoy discovery. My first mission trip ever was just last summer. Our destination was not Haiti, Mexico, or the Appalachian outback. We went to Barcelona, Spain, and had two great weeks of ministry with a small church in a nearby resort town.

Don't get me wrong . . . I'm not an overgrown kid using youth ministry as an excuse for pranks and European travel. It is just that great blocks of time are spent at my desk or with difficult people in my ministry. It is *so nice* to simply enjoy the young people God has given me. This good clean fun is part of personal renewal.

Develop a Healthy Vulnerability. Since we are not perfect and we are just plain human beings, we have problems. Our own needs will be ministered to if we are willing to share them appropriately.

Of course, wisdom is knowing what to share with what groups of people. If your problem is lust, don't share it in junior high Bible study. Hate your senior pastor? Don't lay that burden on your volunteer staff. Many personal problems, though, we can share even with kids and let them support us in prayer. They can understand the frustration of a car that won't stay fixed, problems with our own parents, or ill health.

Never Forget the Kingdom of God Will Always Go On. Continued renewal is possible in our lives when we remember the big picture. In my third year here, I planned a major senior high retreat. I expected seventy, the financial break-even point was fifty, and all of thirty-one actually attended. Furthermore, it was a definite four on a one-to-ten scale in my "retreat memory file." I was discouraged afterward, naturally. But you know, the kingdom of God didn't crumble because of this less than awesome weekend. Through hundreds of ministry mistakes and setbacks over the years, I have managed to learn that the work of God continues unabated in the world.

Yes, I realize we are all theoretically connected in the body of Christ, yet somehow I sense that God's exciting work in Africa, Central America, the next state, or even in the next county is not hurt too much when Mrs. Weasel feels I'm not doing my job right. It's up to me to make sure I'm being sensitive to the needs of the

Mrs. Weasels in my church, but if I fail from time to time, it seems the kingdom manages to lurch ahead anyhow.

Stay in Shape. We have heard dozens of exhortations to keep ourselves healthy physically. It is hard to escape the message that a healthy body facilitates a healthy mind and spirit. Getting regular exercise helps us work off the stress that seems to accumulate in our souls.

In our first years of ministry, we set a pattern that we will likely carry much further into our future. It may be easy to be in shape at age twenty or twenty-two, but we don't have to look at too many thirty-year-old or forty-year-old bodies to see that things change.

Having seen enough obese pastors and youth pastors, at some point in my first few years of ministry I gave myself both a challenge and a goal. My challenge is a lifetime of physical fitness. My goal is to be in better condition physically at ten year intervals. So far, so good. I was in much better shape at age twenty-eight than at age eighteen. At age thirty-eight I was in much better condition than at twenty-eight. Running has been my sport since my twenties, but now it's turned into long-distance running. Those of us who enjoy running, cycling, or aerobic walking receive another benefit: The time can be spent in prayer as well.

Continued personal renewal comes as we keep those extra layers of fat off and avoid nonstop consumption of artery-clogging munchies. I'm no doctor, but I understand that clearer arteries seem to help me have a clearer head.

Steal Like a Bandit. When we see something another youth worker is doing and it looks good . . . try it! The majority of youth workers are not creative geniuses, but competent adapters. It is easy for us to get tunnel vision. This is why it is so important to attend youth ministry seminars and conferences. No, we're not looking for the latest gimmick or sure-fire-money-back-guaranteed program. We are looking, though, for fresh insight, fresh approaches, and encouragement from people who are in the trenches like us.

Nurture Your Inner Life. Last, and most important, is our personal walk with Christ and the refreshment of our spiritual lives. In my first year of ministry, I was lucky to get fifteen to thirty minutes a day for prayer and personal Bible study. There didn't seem to be time for more . . . everything (Bible studies, retreats, administration) took so long to prepare. After the first couple of years, though, it was easier to expand from that meager base.

As youth workers, we face a myriad of obstacles to a deeper walk. There are kids to see, parents to please, retreats to organize, reports to write, and meetings to attend. They are all part of ministry, to be sure. On top of what is normally our job, however, is another reality. The kids may be hard to love; they may be aloof, rude, and content to be selfish pigs. Instead of being supportive, the parents may complain to our face that we are not like our predecessor. Our senior pastor may be so insecure that he or she is starting to speak against us at board meetings. Our spouse may be on us about lack of income or the phone that doesn't stop ringing. We may look in vain for a sector of our universe in which we can rest and find comfort. . . .

That's the way it is sometimes in youth work. And you know, that's okay. Multiple troubles, which yank our rugs of security from under us, force us to look up to him.

The prophet Isaiah probably didn't have youth pastors of the twentieth and twenty-first centuries in mind when he gave the words of the Lord in Isaiah 43:1-2, 4. Yet his words, first addressed to the nation of Israel, are extended to us as believers as well. This is God talking to us . . . and these are words of hope and encouragement. They are words that bring refreshment and renewal to my own spirit when I feel like giving up.

But now, this is what the Lord says—he who created you, O Jacob, he who formed you, O Israel.

We remember that we are made and therefore owned by him. He is our ultimate designer and he made us for this day, this ministry, and this relationship with him.

"Fear not, for I have redeemed you; I have summoned you by name; you are mine."

Fear paralyzes. The Lord exempts us from the inner paralysis of fear because no matter what this battle looks like now, we have already won the war. The Lord knows us specifically, not generically. It refreshes and renews us to realize that his regard for us is not akin to a kind of heavenly class-action lawsuit. The reason we need not fear is that his care is customized for us.

"When you pass through the waters, I will be with you; and when you pass through the rivers, they will not sweep over you. When you walk through the fire, you will not be burned; the flames will not set you ablaze."

In the first few years of ministry we experience many of the disappointments of ministry for the very first time. Trouble makes it seem like we are in deep waters. Seeing the dark side of the church or the underside of people's souls, our ideals may crash and burn on the tarmac of real-life local church ministry. Through the floods and through the fire, the Lord is promising comfort and powerful presence in the middle of our crises.

". . . you are precious and honored in my sight . . . I love you."

Felt in our inner heart or sensed in the hug of a friend, his love floods in to refresh a soul that has been baked dry in the oven of ministry trouble.

We daily admit our weakness and we affirm our wish to cooperate with God's desire to live through us. In doing so, we learn to stay, we learn to hang in there, and we learn to flourish. The result? Continual renewal . . . feeding the spiritual life necessary to make our youth ministry successful in the first years and beyond.

APPENDIX A

SURVEY OF "FIRED" (OR "FORCED RESIGNATION") YOUTH PASTORS

Survey

Please complete this questionnaire to the best of your knowledge. Leave blank those questions about which you have no knowledge.

1. Initials of fired person:_____ Male_____ Female_____
2. Age:_____
3. Married? _____yes _____no
4. College graduate? _____yes _____no
5. Seminary graduate? _____yes _____no
6. Length of his/her ministry at the church:_____
7. Total length in full-time/part-time employed ministry:_____
8. Denomination:_____
9. Size of morning service(s) attendance:_____
10. Numerical growth of the church during the final year of his/her tenure:
    __growth
    __stable
    __decline
    __fluctuated
11. Numerical growth of youth group(s) during the final year of his/her tenure:
    __growth
    __stable
    __decline
    __fluctuated

12. Has this person found another youth ministry (or any ministry) position?

          __yes

          __no

If no, did he/she want one?

          __yes

          __no

13. Reasons for losing job (check as many as apply; please elaborate below, if possible):

    a. ___ Church could no longer afford to pay salary

    b. ___ Senior pastor resigned

    c. ___ Conflict with senior pastor (over what?)

    d. ___ Conflict with church leadership (over what?)

    e. ___ Conflict with parents (over what?)

    f. ___ Conflict with kids (over what?)

    g. ___ Sexual impropriety

    h. ___ Money mishandling

    i. ___ Incompetence (in which areas?)

    j. ___ Addiction (to what?)

    k. ___ Philosophy of ministry difference

    l. ___ Other (please specify)

Your Name:

Results

Sex: 93 percent male
       7 percent female

Age:			
	21-25	17.1	percent
	26-30	41.2	percent
	31-35	26.0	percent
	36-40	12.7	percent
	41-45	3.6	percent

Married?

	Yes	79	percent
	No	11	percent

College Graduate?

	Yes	93	percent
	No	7	percent

Seminary Graduate?

	Yes	34	percent
	No	66	percent

Years at Church:

	1	22.6	percent
	2	31.3	percent
	3	13.0	percent
	4	9.6	percent
	5	12.0	percent
	6	3.5	percent
	7	0.9	percent
	8+	7.0	percent

Total Ministry Years:

	1-5	42.4	percent
	6-10	37.4	percent

11-15	14.2	percent
16+	5.0	percent

Denomination:

Baptist	21.9	percent
Independent	14.9	percent
Christian and Missionary Alliance	14.0	percent
Nazarene	13.2	percent
Lutheran	12.3	percent
Assemblies	6.1	percent
Other	6.1	percent
Presbyterian	4.4	percent
Covenant	1.8	percent

Size of Morning Worship:

Under 100	3	percent
100-199	12	percent
200-299	18	percent
300-399	13	percent
400-499	10	percent
500-599	7	percent
600-699	4	percent
700-799	6	percent
800+	25	percent

Church Growth in Final Year of Youth Pastor's Tenure:

growth	35	percent
stable	42	percent
decline	18	percent
fluctuated	5	percent

Youth Group Growth in Final Year of Youth Pastor's Tenure:

growth	42	percent
stable	39	percent

decline	14	percent
fluctuated	5	percent

Found Another Youth Ministry Position?

Yes	48	percent
No	52	percent

If No, Did He/She Want One?

Yes	35	percent
No	65	percent

Reason for Firing:

Church ran out of money	9.4	percent
Senior pastor resigned	10.3	percent
Conflict with senior pastor	41.9	percent
Conflict with church leadership	27.4	percent
Conflict with parents	17.9	percent
Conflict with kids	8.5	percent
Sexual impropriety	14.5	percent
Money mishandling	1.0	percent
Incompetence	19.7	percent
Addiction	2.6	percent
Philosophy of ministry difference	18.8	percent
Other	19.7	percent

SAMPLE SCHEDULES

'Wednesday Ministry (Schedule for Staff)
Special Topics

Topic	Opening	Teaching	2nd Half	Gym?
January				
3 Prophecy	Team Mtg.	Len	Len	Y
10 Reach Out Ministries (visit nursing home; bake cookies for elderly; visit absentees; write letters to missionary kids)				N
17 New Age	Len	Mike	Mike	Y
24 Missions Focus	Len	Guest	Len	N
31 Special Outreach Led by Cabinet: Theme—Friends				
February				
7 If God is Good, Why Suffering?	Len	Mike	Mike	N
14 Special Outreach Led by Team Leaders: Theme—Love				
21 Reach Out Ministries				N
28 "Nieve/LukeWarm" Mike	Len	Len	Y	
March				
7 Devotional Life	Len	Mike	Mike	N
14 Reach Out Ministries				N
21 Special Outreach Led by Cabinet: Theme—Purpose			Y	
27 Evolution	Mike	Len	Len	Y

**Senior High Sunday School
Spring Quarter 1991**

March 3–May 28, 1991

Time to think about spring quarter and which elective you think will best meet your needs. Here is a short rundown of the six electives. Fill out the form below, indicating your first, second, and third choices. Give to Jeff Shdo on Sunday or Wednesday. Space is limited in some classes; first to register get priority.

ELECTIVE 1   "The Book of Esther." So . . . whadaya know about this little Old Testament book? There's lots to learn. Led by Bill Maxson.

ELECTIVE 2   "Piercing the Darkness." Using Frank Peretti's novel as a source for learning what the Bible says about spiritual warfare and the new-age movement. Book is $10. Bring money on March 3. This course has homework. Led by Jeff and Len.

ELECTIVE 3   "Radical for the King." Studies the life of Christ and how to impact our world like he did. Cost for workbook is $5. Bring money on March 3. Led by Peggy Gerdes.

ELECTIVE 4   "I Hate to Witness." Yep . . . sometimes we don't know what to say or do, but we know we should do something. Here's some practical help. Led by Joanna Fuller and Sara Richey.

ELECTIVE 5   Two Mini-Courses: "Friends: Finding and Keeping" and "Help: Coping with Crises." Practical, fun, biblical. Led by Dan and Lynn Bleeker.

ELECTIVE 6   Children's Ministry. Be a Bible school assis-
              tant in children's ministry for the quarter.

Senior High Bible School Electives

Place a "1" by your first choice, a "2" by your second, and a "3" by
your third. If you select courses that cost money, be sure to bring
the right amount on March 3.

Your Name: _____

              ELECTIVE 1 ___   "The Book of Esther"
                               (Bill Maxson)
              ELECTIVE 2 ___   "Piercing the Darkness"
                               (Jeff and Len)
              ELECTIVE 3 ___   "Radical for the King"
                               (Peggy Gerdes)
              ELECTIVE 4 ___   "I Hate to Witness"
                               (Joanna Fuller and Sara Richey)
              ELECTIVE 5 ___   "Friends" and "Crises"
                               (Dan and Lynn Bleeker)
              ELECTIVE 6 ___   Help in Children's Bible School

Senior High Night Life Calendar
(For Parents' Information)
January–March 1991

<u>January</u>
12	(Sat)	9:00 a.m.–4:00 p.m.	Inner Tubing at Snoq. Pass Chris Kertson
21	(Mon)	6:45 a.m.–6:30 p.m.	Skiing at Stevens Len Kageler
27	(Sun)	7:15 p.m.–9:00 p.m.	Cemetery Search Jeff Shdo

<u>February</u>
3	(Sun)	12:30 p.m.–4:00 p.m.	Rain-or-Shine Gasworks Park Play Day Brent Kroon
9	(Sat)	6:45 a.m.–6:30 p.m.	Skiing at Stevens Jeff Shdo
16–18	(Sat-Mon)		District Youth Congress Chris Kertson
22	(Fri)	6:00 p.m.–10:30 p.m.	Celebrate Life '91 at Overlake Christian Church Chris Kertson

<u>March</u>
2	(Sat)	7:00 p.m.–10:00 p.m.	Bowling and Pizza Dan and Lynn Bleeker
3	(Sun)	To Be Announced	Missions Banquet
9	(Sat)	6:30 p.m.–10:30 p.m.	Swimming, Gym,and Exercise Machine Night: Bellevue YMCA Jeff Shdo
16	(Sat)	10:00 a.m.–2:00 p.m.	The Zoo in Early Spring Mike Wood
24	(Sun)	7:15 p.m.–9:30 p.m.	Blind Date Night with Westminster Chapel Chris Kertson

Who's Doing What Flow Sheet (For Staff)
January–March 1991

January
   12 (Sat) 9:00 a.m.–4:00 p.m.   Inner Tubing, Snoq. Pass
                                     TBSH* Chris
                                     Bus Driving
                                     Extra Staff
   21 (Mon) 6:45 a.m.–6:30 p.m.   Skiing at Stevens
                                     TBSH Len
                                     Bus Driving
                                     Extra Staff
   27 (Sun) 7:15 p.m.–9:00 p.m.   Cemetery Search
                                       TBSH Jeff
                                     Bus Driving
                                     Extra Staff

February
    3 (Sun) 12:30 p.m.–4:00 p.m.   Playing at Gasworks
                                       TBSH Brent
                                     Bus Driving
                                     Extra Staff
    9 (Sat) 6:45 a.m.–6:30 p.m.   Skiing at Stevens
                                         TBSH Jeff
                                     Bus Driving
                                     Extra Staff
16–18 (Sat-Mon)   District Youth Congress
                                     TBSH Chris
                                     Bus Driving
                                     Staff
   22 (Fri) 6:00 p.m.–10:30 p.m.   Celebrate Life '91 at
                                       Overlake
                                     TBSH Chris
                                     Bus Driving
                                     Extra Staff

March
    2 (Sat) 7:00 p.m.–10:00 p.m.   Bowling and Pizza with a
                                       Missionary
                                       TBSH Team 1

			Bus Driving
			Extra Staff
3	(Sun)	To Be Announced	Missions Banquet
			TBSH
			Bus Driving
			Extra Staff
9	(Sat)	6:30 p.m.–10:30 p.m.	Bellevue YMCA Night
			TBSH Jeff
			Bus Driving
			Extra Staff
16	(Sat)	10:00 a.m.–2:00 p.m.	Woodlawn Park Zoo
			TBSH Team 2
			Bus Driving
			Extra Staff
24	(Sun)	7:15 p.m.–9:30 p.m.	Blind Date Night
			TBSH Chris
			Bus Driving
			Extra Staff

*TBSH means "The Buck Stops Here"

SIX-YEAR
CURRICULUM PLAN

**Junior and Senior High Midweek Ministries
North Seattle Alliance Church**

Junior High

Year One
Fall	Philippians
Winter	Topics
Spring	1 and 2 Peter
Summer	Old Testament People

Year Two
Fall	Romans 12–16
Winter	Topics
Spring	1 and 2 Thessalonians
Summer	Proverbs

Senior High

Year One
Fall	James
Winter	Topics
Spring	1 and 2 Corinthians
Summer	1 and 2 Samuel

Year Two
Fall	Romans
Winter	Topics
Spring	Romans
Summer	Psalms

Year Three
    Fall   Matthew 5–7
    Winter   Topics
    Spring   Hebrews
    Summer   Genesis

Year Four
    Fall   1 and 2 Timothy
    Winter   Topics
    Spring   Ephesians
    Summer   Amos

Note: (a) Gospels are part of Sunday morning curriculum; (b) Every paragraph of every chapter is not necessarily covered. In any given chapter, we may focus on only a couple of verses that are most relevant to the young people.

Sample Quarter: Senior High/First Year/Fall

DATE	TEXT	KEY FOCUS VERSES

September

11	James 1:2–8	2–5
18	James 1:9–18	13–15
25	James 1:19–27	21–24

October

2	Youth-led Outreach Program: Theme—Parents	
9	James 2:1–13	1–7
16	James 2:14–26	14–18
23	Service Project Night	
30	James 3:1–12	1–3

November

6	James 3:13–18	17–18
13	Senior highers combine with adult prayer meeting	
20	James 4:1–6	1–3
27	No meeting: Thanksgiving service next day	

December

4	James 4:7–10	all
11	Youth-led Outreach Program: Theme—Giving	
18 and 25	Christmas break: no Wednesday night programs	

YOUTH SURVEY (FALL)

Name:

Year You Graduate:

Team Number:

Below are several items related to your life and your walk with God. Tell us how you are doing.

> 1 = I'm doing okay.
> 2 = I'd like some help on this.
> 3 = I urgently want help with this; please call as soon as possible!

My Walk with God

___ 1. Making progress in my relationship with God.

___ 2. Having a regular time to read the Bible and think about him.

___ 3. Praying regularly and effectively.

___ 4. Knowing for certain that I'm a Christian and that I will go to heaven when I die.

My Attitude Toward Serving Him

___ 5. Deciding what to do when I grow up.

___ 6. Knowing what my spiritual gifts are.

___ 7. Being committed to serving him in this group and church.

___ 8. Willingness to help other people, even non-Christians, in whatever way I can.

My Own Life and Lifestyle

___ 9. Feeling good about how I look.
___ 10. Learning to evaluate my schedule and time priorities.
___ 11. Handling money.
___ 12. Fulfilling responsibilities, being dependable.
___ 13. Being willing to look beyond my own needs and wants.
___ 14. Having social skills (starting conversations, meeting new people, feeling comfortable socially).

Witness and Mission

___ 15. Having confidence in sharing Christ with my friends.
___ 16. Knowing how to defend my faith.
___ 17. Caring about the salvation of others here and around the world.

Discipling

___ 18. Feeling that I've been discipled.
___ 19. Knowing how to disciple someone else.

Family and Friends

___ 20. Being able to have close friends.
___ 21. Being able to have right relationships with boys/girls.
___ 22. Being part of the solution, not part of the problem in my family.
___ 23. Being a good example of what a Christian is among my friends and people in general.

PERFORMANCE APPRAISAL QUESTIONNAIRE

For:_____

Date Completed:_____

Enclosed are questions aimed at identifying some of the numerous factors that make for an effective pastoral staff member at North Seattle Alliance Church. Those being evaluated are interested in improving their ministry and service to people.

This form is being completed by several persons. Your ratings will be grouped with others and only composite results will be seen by the person being evaluated. The composite will also be reviewed by the Personnel Committee of the Governing Board, with results reported to the full board.

Please do not sign this form. You may return it in the envelope provided. If it is not returned within two weeks, it will be assumed that you do not wish to participate.

I feel I know this person: ___very little (in that case, please do not answer questionnaire)
___somewhat
___well
___very well

Public impression (circle any applicable description and comment if you wish):

General Appearance: neat, sloppy, good taste, poor taste, striking, average

Voice: too fast, too slow, good variety, good diction, poor diction, monotonous

Posture: stiff, athletic, slumped, erect, controlled

Facial Expression: accepting, severe, dignified, serious, happy, unhappy

Please rate as many as possible of the following items, using this scale:

    1 = superior, outstanding

    2 = good, above average

    3 = average, adequate, could be strengthened

    4 = poor, inadequate

    n/a = not applicable; insufficient knowledge for rating

Space is provided for comments under each heading; they are especially encouraged if a "3" or "4" rating is given.

___ 1. Provides spiritual leadership for those who look to him/her.

___ 2. Has rapport with those with whom he/she works.

___ 3. Is positive and equitable in relationships with other staff members.

___ 4. Is sensitive to the varied needs of people at all levels of experience and background.

___ 5. Is open to input from others in recommending and maintaining reasonable standards.

___ 6. Helps to provide an atmosphere where all are encouraged to "share one another's burdens."

___ 7. Is fair in dealing with people in conflict situations.

___ 8. Avoids exchange of derogatory remarks with others.

___ 9. Helps people set and achieve meaningful goals.

___10. Lets me know when I do a good job.

___11. Inspires interest in improving the church program.

___12. Encourages me to try new methods and approaches in my work for Christ.

___13. Appears to keep a proper balance between his/her church work and extra church activity, including family time.

___14. Provides clear and consistent directions.

___15. Does not make unreasonable demands on my time.

___16. Respects and seeks to know my individual characteristics, talents, and potentials.

___17. Treats me as a responsible person.

___18. Gives people freedom of action within their proper sphere to do God's work in their own style.

___19. Evaluates me fairly, both formally and informally.

___20. Has the ability and courage to give constructive criticism in a friendly, firm, and positive manner.

___21. Encourages and helps me in the development of my spiritual gifts and ministries.

___22. Is hospitable to my opinions—whether solicited or volunteered—and considers them fairly and without prejudice.

___23. Openly accepts suggestions and implements them where workable.

___24. Is resourceful in coping with problems.

___25. Reflects willingness to share and counsel with me about spiritual concerns.

___26. Demonstrates leadership in practical and spiritual ways.

___27. Anticipates problems.

___28. Is accessible when needed.

___29. Is a team player, as opposed to a "lone ranger."

___30. Appears to work by established priorities.

___31. Appears not to be overwhelmed by a volume of lesser tasks.

___32. Is perceived to be fully committed to NSA Church, its people and its purposes.

___33. Is approachable: I would gladly seek his/her help in solving a personal problem.

___34. Serves as an effective modeler of Christian behavior and attitude.

___35. Appears knowledgeable and competent in his/her area of ministry.

___36. Does not display outward impatience/irritation with people or programs that may be delaying progress.

___37. Keeps his/her word on commitments; is faithful.

Fill out 38-40 if you have had adequate opportunity to observe the individual's preaching ministry.

___38. Presents ideas clearly and understandably.
___39. Is able to make Scripture applicable to my life.
___40. Seems to enjoy preaching.

Please complete 41-46 if you have had adequate opportunity to observe the individual's teaching ministry.

___41. Presents ideas clearly and understandably.
___42. Encourages discussion.
___43. Is able to keep things on track without being rigid or inflexible.
___44. Handles distractions and/or discipline.
___45. Is able to make material applicable to my life.
___46. Seems to enjoy teaching.

* * *

___47. Demonstrates overall competence and organization.
___48. I have confidence in him/her.
___49. I have respect for, and confidence in, his/her judgment.

Thank you for your investment of time and interest in this individual's ministry.

ENDNOTES

CHAPTER TWO

1. Adapted from notes taken at a Fred Pryor "Leadership Skills" seminar, Seattle, Wash., April 18, 1981. For further information contact Fred Pryor Seminars, 5909 Martway, Mission, KS, 66202.
2. For more information about Seasonal Affective Disorder, see: Norman Rosenthal, *Seasonal Affective Disorders and Phototherapy* (New York: Guilford Press, 1989); *Journal of the American Medical Association* 259 (February 19, 1988): 958; *Scientific American* 260 (January 1989): 68; *Sports Illustrated* (December 21, 1987), 21; *Vogue* (February 1990), 230.
3. "Sizing Up SADness According to Latitude," *Science News* 136 (September 23, 1989): 198.

CHAPTER THREE

1. *The American College Dictionary* (New York: Random House, 1969), 254.
2. Dub Ambrose, "Is It Possible to Team Up with Your Pastor?" *Youthworker* 4, no. 4 (Winter 1988): 50.
3. James Dobson, *Parenting Isn't for Cowards* (Waco, Tex.: Word, 1987), 36.
4. Len Kageler, *Teen Shaping: Solving the Discipline Dilemma* (Old Tappan, N.J.: Revell, 1990), 72.

CHAPTER FOUR

1. *Youthworker* 7, no. 2 (Fall 1990): 56-57.
2. *Leadership* 9, no. 1 (Winter 1988): 12-13.
3. *Youthworker* 7, no. 2 (Fall 1990).

CHAPTER FIVE

1. Robert Hochheiser, *How To Work for a Jerk* (New York: Random House, 1987), Preface.
2. I have adapted the first five of these questions from an address that Larry Richards gave at North American Baptist Seminary, Sioux Falls, S.D., in 1975.
3. See Daniel J. Levinson, *The Seasons of a Man's Life* (New York: Knopf, 1978). This book is exclusively about men.
4. Jean Lush, *The Emotional Phases of a Woman's Life* (Old Tappan, N.J.: Revell, 1988).
5. Anthony Campolo, *Growing Up in America* (Grand Rapids: YS/Zondervan, 1989), 170.
6. Campolo, 170-72.
7. Dub Ambrose, "Is It Possible to Team Up with Your Pastor?" *Youthworker* 4, no. 4 (Winter 1988): 50-56.

CHAPTER SIX

1. Martha Farnsworth Riche, "People Talk," *The Wall Street Journal* (October 2, 1990), B1(W).
2. James Dobson, *Parenting Isn't for Cowards* (Waco, Tex.: Word, 1987), 13.
3. Richard Bolles, *What Color Is Your Parachute?* (Berkeley: Ten Speed Press, 1983), 16.
4. Bolles, 15.
5. Jean Lush, *The Emotional Phases of a Woman's Life* (Old Tappan, N.J.: Revell, 1988).
6. Gina Kolata, "Mothers with Dark Circles," *The New York Times Book Review* (June 25, 1989): 3.
7. Martha Farnsworth Riche, "No Time for Kids," *American Demographics* 12 (June 1990): 13.
8. A Conversation with Dr. Merton Strommen, "The Five Cries of Parents," *Youthworker* 2, no. 1 (Spring 1985): 51.
9. Paul Thigpen, "Layin' Your (Parental) Burden Down," *Youthworker* 2, no. 1 (Spring 1985): 62-68.
10. Jim Walton, "Ministry To Parents," *Youthworker* 2, no. 1 (Spring 1985): 70-72.

11. Jay Kesler, *Parents and Teenagers* (Wheaton, Ill.: Victor, 1984).
12. Written by a parent committee of North Seattle Alliance Church with youth pastors Len Kageler and Chris Kertson (Fall 1989).

CHAPTER EIGHT

1. For a full discussion of this, see former President Reagan's chief media consultant, Roger Ailes, *You Are the Message* (Homewood, Ill.: Dow Jones Irwin Press, 1988).
2. Youth socials are out of favor in the minds of some because it is better, they say, to spend our time in more spiritual and focused ways. The socials we have are a definite part of our philosophy of ministry. For us, they are an arena in which (1) our core kids can invite non-Christian friends so they'll get comfortable with the group and be more likely to come back on a Wednesday night; (2) our core kids reach out to young people on the periphery of the group; and (3) our volunteer staff can build relationships.
3. Larry Richards, *Creative Bible Teaching* (Chicago: Moody Press, 1970).
4. Watchman Nee, *The Normal Christian Life* (London: Victory Press, 1961).

CHAPTER NINE

1. Kenneth Blanchard, *The One Minute Manager* (New York: Morrow, 1982).
2. Adapted from Walter Kiechel, III, "How Executives Think," *Fortune* (February 4, 1985), 127-28.
3. Kiechel.

MANAGEMENT RESOURCES

Kenneth Blanchard, *The One Minute Manager* (New York: Morrow,1982); Edward R. Dayton and Ted W. Engstrom, *The Christian Executive* (Waco, Tex.: Word, 1979); Robert Mager, *Goal Analysis* (Belmont, Calif.: Fearon Publishers, 1972); George S. Odiorne, *Management by Objectives* (New York: Pitman Publishing Corp., 1985); Thomas J. Peters and Robert

Waterman, *In Search of Excellence* (New York: Harper and Row, 1982); Fred Pryor, "Managing People," a one-day seminar. For information, write 5909 Martway, Mission, KS 66202.

CHAPTER TEN

1. Richard L. Bergstrom, "Stunned by an Inside Job," *Leadership* 8, no. 1 (Winter 1987): 102-03.
2. "*Youthworker* Roundtable: Facing Your Sexual Struggles," *Youthworker* 1, no. 4 (Winter 1985): 29.
3. "*Youthworker* Roundtable: Facing Your Sexual Struggles," 30.
4. Gordon MacDonald, *Rebuilding Your Broken World* (Nashville: Nelson, 1988).
5. MacDonald, 97, 105, 117, 129, and 140.
6. Randy Alcorn, "Strategies to Keep from Falling," *Leadership* 9, no. 1 (Winter 1988): 42-47. See especially the box on p. 46, entitled "Consequences of a Moral Tumble."

CHAPTER ELEVEN

1. Mike Yaconelli and Jim Burns, *High School Ministry* (Grand Rapids: YS/Zondervan, 1986), 114; Warren S. Benson and Mark H. Senter, eds., *The Complete Book of Youth Ministry* (Chicago: Moody Press, 1987), described on p. 227; Dann Spader, *SonLife Strategy of Youth Discipleship and Evangelism* (SonLife Ministries, 1119 Wheaton Oaks Ct., Wheaton, IL 60187).
2. Les Christie, *How to Recruit and Train Volunteer Youth Workers* (Grand Rapids: YS/Zondervan, 1991). Previously published as *Unsung Heroes* (1987).

CHAPTER TWELVE

1. Diane Cole, "Fired, But Not Frantic," *Psychology Today* 22 (May 1988): 25.
2. Elisabeth Kubler-Ross, *On Death and Dying* (New York: Macmillan, 1969).
3. Carrie Leana and Daniel Feldman, "Individual Response to Job Loss: Perceptions, Reactions, Coping Behaviors," *Journal of Management* 14 (September 1988): 376.